KAHLIL
GIBRAN

AN ILLUSTRATED ANTHOLOGY

KAHLIL
GIBRAN

AN ILLUSTRATED ANTHOLOGY

Ayman A El-Desouky

DEDICATION

To the spirit of my father, Ahmed El-Desouky, for
his time runs through my body, a jolt of essence,
a glow of ether, a passion for life!

An Hachette UK Company
First published in Great Britain in 2010 by Spruce
a division of Octopus Publishing Group Limited
Endeavour House, 189 Shaftesbury Avenue, London, WC2H 8JY

www.octopusbooks.co.uk
www.octopusbooksusa.com

Distributed in the Canada for Octopus Books USA
c/- Hachette Book Group USA
237 Park Avenue
New York NY 10017

ISBN 13 978-1-84601-338-6
ISBN 10 1-84601-338-0

A catalogue record for this book is available from the
British Library

This book contains the opinions and ideas of the author. It is intended
to provide helpful and informative material on the subjects addressed
in this book and is sold with the understanding that the author and
publisher are not engaged in rendering any kind of personal professional
services in this book.

CONTENTS

Introduction
Gibran, A Self-Begetting Modern?

Detail from *Face of Almustafa* (frontispiece for *The Prophet*), 1923, Charcoal, 15½ x 18½ inches (47 x 39.5 cm) Gibran Museum, Bisharri, Lebanon

WITH THE PUBLICATION of his most famous work, *The Prophet*, in 1923, Kahlil Gibran began to receive the recognition he had long desired in the West. He wished for more than fame, longing to be acknowledged as a spiritual teacher and inspirational speaker. As a prophet, Gibran felt he had a new and hopeful message for humanity: that we can all realize our potential, or access the god-like self, latent within each of us. By the time he moved to New York in 1912, Gibran was already being recognized in the Arab world as a Romantic poet. Indeed, he stood at the forefront of the new poetic sensibility that had begun to emerge on the Arab scene at the turn of the 20th century, particularly in Egypt and the Levant. Between New York and the Arab world, Gibran's twinned destiny—as a prophet in English and a poet in Arabic—was unfolding.

Gibran struggled to articulate these two different but related senses of self and destiny in his writing, just as he strove to tally them in his personal life. Even so, in the West, it is Gibran the prophet who has mostly survived, at the expense of Gibran the artist and poet. In the Arab East, it is Gibran of *The Processions* from 1919 and of other poems, critical essays and short stories who is better known, to the detriment of Gibran the artist and prophet; at least until recently. By the 1960s, Gibran's works were being reprinted and translated, given impetus by the New Age movement, and they finally became available to a wider readership in English, Arabic and many other languages. Indeed, in Spanish, Gibran's work is now more accessible than *The Arabian Nights*!

But it is Kahlil Gibran the artist who has suffered most from lack of recognition. Gibran started out as an unschooled but highly talented technician with an acute awareness of the conceptual and symbolic power of the image. This aspect of his creative personality drew the attention of his early benefactors and mentors in Boston. The artist and pioneering conceptual photographer Fred Holland Day was the first to take the young Gibran under his wing, introducing him to the worlds of

TITLE PAGE *Self Portrait and Muse*, 1911, Color litho, Kahlil Gibran (1883–1931), Private Collection

art, music and high society, which were vibrant in turn-of-the-century Boston. Day also encouraged the young artist's sense of destiny, alongside Gibran's first muse, the Bostonian poet Josephine Preston Peabody. But it was Gibran's life-long benefactress Mary Haskell, his "She-Angel," to whom he was introduced by Josephine, who decided that Gibran should pursue his artistic education more systematically, and who offered to finance a two-year trip to Paris. Here, between 1908 and 1910, Gibran's early impulses guided him toward symbolic and allegorical methods—one of the reviewers of his first exhibition in Wellesley College, Massachusetts, in 1903 had already mentioned similarities with William Blake's work, foreshadowing the later reception of Gibran's art. In Paris, under the influence of sculptor Auguste Rodin and the wider art scene, he began to articulate his impulses more consciously. The famous "Temple of Art" series of portraits was conceived in Paris; he would draw, mostly in pencil (his favorite medium), artists and world-historical figures of past and present. The series included some of his most famous contemporaries, including Carl Jung, Rabindranath Tagore and W. B. Yeats, who sat for him. Others, such as Rodin, he most likely copied from photographs. Gibran also produced imaginative portraits of Arab poets and philosophers from the 10th century.

Gibran conceived his paintings and drawings largely as he did his writings, around a single, central vision or thought. He then rendered and refined this vision either into single drawings or paintings, or short pieces of prose. In all media, Gibran aimed to invoke a powerful and transformative thought or emotion in the reader or viewer, whether through the movement of words or of the beholding eye. He admired Leonardo da Vinci because he, too, "painted mind. He wanted to paint what men could not understand." This insight, which Mary Haskell recorded in her Journal on 30 August 1913, explains the basic impulse behind Gibran's art, especially in the early phase, when reviewers

66 *The Prophet…is my rebirth and my first baptism, the only thought in me that will make me worthy to stand in the light of the sun. For this prophet had already 'written' me before I attempted to 'write' him, had created me before I created him…* 99

9 November 1919

frequently commented on the work's ambiguities and vagueness of expression. Gibran thought highly of Michelangelo, too, for creating heroic "Superman" figures who were at once physical male and human god. There are other clear influences on his art: Eugène Carrière's fluid figures and Rodin's sculptures are evident in Gibran's many exquisite renditions of the body. He also appreciated the work of Titian and Velázquez. But William Blake had the most profound impact on Gibran. He impressed him on many levels, as poet and prophet as well as allegorical and symbolic artist. The largest surviving body of Gibran's paintings and drawings is those he prepared as illustrations for his writing, but there were many exhibitions of his work between Boston and New York, such as the famous "Centaur" series, about forty works in all, which was shown in New York in 1918 and in Boston in 1919. This is perhaps the best visual representation of Gibran's belief that the human condition can be understood as a process of evolution toward a higher self.

In this volume I hope to offer a rounded vision of Gibran the man, the artist and the poet-prophet. The aim is to "reclaim" Gibran for the modern reader, to beckon Gibran the man and Gibran the creator out of the confinement of particular histories of reception that have reduced his personality and his work to boxes: the Prophet of the New Age, the Romantic Poet of early modern Arabic verse, the sentimental writer and soft spiritualist who "had his heyday in the 1960s and is now read by those who do not read poetry!," as the former Poet Laureate Andrew Motion once remarked to me during a relaxed chat over dinner. This is a view shared by many contemporary Western poets, who have a hard time accepting Gibran's style of English and his expressions of simple wisdom. Technically speaking, Gibran wrote very few poems. They are entirely in Arabic and are boldly experimental, but such rich explorations of form, diction and imagery could only be appreciated by someone steeped in the history of Arabic poetry. This has as long and almost as sacred a history as the high art of the Arabs, and is the highest repository of the riches of the Arabic language after the Qur'an. For Gibran, a poet must be a singer not an artificer of words or a cold purveyor of the world of the intellect. Neither should he be a poet of occasion, which was the norm among his contemporary Neoclassical Arab poets. Gibran's most radical influence on modern Arabic poetry was to shift the form from poetry as high art to poetry as an expression of the poet's soul. He dared to use everyday words, not to mention striking natural imagery, Greco-Roman mythology and a biblical voice and syntax. The Gibran that modern poets in the West have in mind is the American Gibran, a crafter of simplistic language, but the power of his English lies precisely in the simplicity of his style and expression, which is a manifestation of his vision for a new way of living. On the Arab scene, Gibran's significance is largely regarded as historical. He is thought of as a Romantic poet and figurehead of the influential *Mahjar* or Expatriate School, represented by the Pen Club or *Arrabitah*, which he helped to found in New York in 1920, with fellow expatriate Arab poets and writers.

GIBRAN, THE SELF-BEGETTING MODERN

Between the years 1850 and 1950, a new phenomenon appeared in the history of Western literature: a breed of semi-autobiographical "begetters." These fictive creations embodied their authors's visions of their own potential, and through them writers attempted to transcend the limitations of their personalities and eras. The characters include Walt Whitman's "Walt Whitman," Friedrich Nietzsche's Zarathustra, James Joyce's Stephen Dedalus, Fernando Pessoa's Alberto Caeiro, Rainer Maria Rilke's Angel, Baron Corvo's Whole Person, Nikos Kazantzakis's Odysseus and, of course, Kahlil Gibran's Prophet. These figures are not just the principal fictional characters in their authors's works, they demonstrate a new way of living that emerged when the writer used his creativity to explore and recover from unendurable personal or historical circumstances. The author begins to encounter himself as an enigma and to inhabit possibility as the ground of creativity and genuine individuality. For the young Gibran, it was alienation from the safety and beauty of his native Bisharri in Lebanon, his long experience of poverty, and the personal tragedy of the death of his sister Sultana, half-brother Peter and mother, all within the short span of fifteen months—not to mention his profound creative struggles and the battle to fulfil his sense of his own destiny.

Detail from *The Great Longing*, c.1916, Watercolor and pencil on paper, 8½ x 10⅞ inches (27.6 × 21.6 cm), The Telfair Museum of Art, Savannah, Georgia

Detail from *The Divine World*
(illustration for *The Prophet*),
1923, Charcoal, 8½ x 11 inches
(28 x 21.6 cm) Gibran Museum,
Bisharri, Lebanon

In Paris, Gibran discovered Nietzsche and his Zarathustra, and, inspired by them, began to express himself more forcefully and engage with historical issues. He reflected on many aspects of capitalism and modern industrial life in America, but also on more immediate political causes, such as the call for Home Rule in the Ottoman territories, including his native land, and on social injustice the world over. As a creator with a vision and an indomitable will to beget, Gibran wished to reforge many of the social, political and religious aspects of contemporary life to better suit an individual seeking to fulfil his or her potential. In this, he was inspired by Jesus, of whom he began to think more profoundly when in Paris, gestating what would later become the key tenet of his 1928 work *Jesus, the Son of Man*—Christ's humanity. Gibran felt he was finally finding the right voice and form of expression, and began to offer up role models in his writing and drawings. All Gibran's memorable characters—Khalil the Heretic, Yuhanna the Madman, The Poet, The Madman, The Forerunner and The Wanderer— are rebellious but profoundly human figures who attempt to coax the creative self out of the reader or viewer. They culminated in the Prophet and Jesus the Man, who would reveal this new way of being to everyone, including Gibran himself.

I find this quote from Nikos Kazantzakis's autobiography *Report to Greco* a telling account (even a self-conscious parable) of this peculiarly modern experience of creative "self-begetting." The deeply personal epiphany appears toward the end of the book and connects the trajectory of Kazantzakis's life with the personal struggle of his literary career up to the moment of writing *Odysseus* (the italics are my own):

"All the routes of the mind led to the abyss. My youth and maturity had revolved in the air around the two poles of panic and hope, but now in my old age I stood before the abyss tranquilly, fearlessly. I no longer fled, no longer humiliated myself—no, not I, but the Odysseus I was fashioning. *I created him to face the abyss calmly, and in creating him, I strove to resemble him. I myself was being created. I entrusted all my own yearnings to this Odysseus; he was the mould I was carving out so that the man of the future might flow in. Whatever I yearned for and was unable to attain, he would attain. He was the charm that would lure the tenebrous and luminous forces that create the future.* Faith moves mountains; believe in him and he would come. Who would come? The Odysseus I had created. He was the Archetype."

Kazantzakis's Odysseus is a semi-autobiographical creation, fashioned out of a particular personal history and creative struggle. But this Odysseus is also a vision of a possible self. It enables its author to "face the abyss calmly" by offering him a chance to reconfigure experience, yearning and ambition "so that the man of the future might flow in." This man of the future is a uniquely modern human type and a model still for all who "seek themselves."

Each of the authors and thinkers I have mentioned has forged new forms of expression and a profoundly personal voice from a keen sense of vocation. Kazantzakis sought to redeem not only himself, but his entire race, like Nietzsche's Zarathustra, who wants to hammer out the images sleeping in the rough stone that men have become to allow "the image of [his] vision" to emerge. The "Walt Whitman" of the poems seeks to create a society of perfect counterparts to the vision of his own soul, while Joyce's Stephen Dedalus dreams of offering his vision as the word made flesh in his readers. Just as the figure of the self-begetter mediates between the writer and his higher self, so these writers mediate between the reader and his or her possible future.

Gibran, too, had a heightened sense of personal vocation. In a strikingly prescient statement, similar in sentiment and impulse to Kazantzakis's thoughts, Gibran wrote to his beloved May Ziadeh in Cairo on 9 November 1919, "*The Prophet*...is my rebirth and my first baptism, the only thought in me that will make me worthy to stand in the light of the sun. For this prophet had already 'written' me before I attempted to 'write' him, had created me before I created him, and had silently set me on a course to follow him for seven thousand leagues before he appeared in front of me to dictate his wishes and inclinations." This strong sense of himself and his destiny helps to account for Gibran's personal eccentricities, as well as his achievements, and for the attraction his persona held for others.

> " I am indebted for all that I call 'I' to women, ever since I was an infant. Women opened the windows of my eyes and the doors of my spirit. "
>
> 1928

Gibran was only too aware of his own vocation and creative impulses. "Invention is the only thing, with me—the pushing out through one's own skin, projecting one's own self," he explained to Mary on 10 September 1920. But was there a philosophy behind them? Some have claimed he was influenced by the pantheism of the Andalusian philosopher-mystic Ibn Arabi, the theologian-mystic al-Ghazali, the poet-mystic Ibn al-Farid and others from the Arabic and Islamic traditions who gripped his early imagination and sensibilities. Others have seen him as a belated Romantic in the tradition of the American transcendentalists such as Ralph Waldo Emerson, Henry David Thoreau and Walt Whitman. Or was he a Theosophist? A Nietzschean? A French Symbolist?

The fundamental impulses that sparked Gibran's creative expression could be briefly listed as follows: rebelliousness, an attraction to the numinous, a concern for freedom and the individual, and an urge to personify absolute values in the present world. Let's look first at his rebelliousness. What did Gibran rebel against? Firstly, convention, oppressive traditions and society's norms. For instance, he refused to participate in national politics later in life back in Lebanon, on the grounds of being suspicious of state institutions and in favor of a more person-based politics. He also rebelled against everything he deemed to be ephemeral, contingent, accidental, historical, man-made or reversible. He was against the divisions, traditions and institutions of organized religion, particularly monotheistic religions, and for the oneness of everything in origin and spirit.

In his 1905 treatise *On Music*, his first extended creative piece, Gibran explored his attraction to the numinous, or anything that inspires a spiritual response. In this piece, Gibran stated that melodies form a wordless language of the spirit that supports self-reflection and dialogue with others. One is reminded of philosopher Arthur Schopenhauer's view of music as the "thing in itself." Gibran viewed nature in much the same way. His early responses to music and to the beauty and peace of the natural world seem to have formed Gibran's compulsion to seek what is beyond the visible—the numinous truths. This drove him to peculiar forms of expression in language and art. In his writing, Gibran had a natural inclination toward the fragmentary and the gesturing phrase that reveals his inner workings. He was also convinced that what is unsaid must remain silent: in almost all his artwork, a rather shadowy abstract figure appears in the background. He was suspicious of ready-made forms—laws, practices, mores, institutions—regarding them as oppressive impositions from outside. This is indicative of his modernist impulse toward freedom and the individual. He preferred to turn set beliefs, from mythologies to the institution of marriage, into the stuff of poetry. By representing abstract values as characters in his writing and engaging them in dialogue or subjecting them to circumstance, random events and human contradictions, Gibran gave his readers space to reflect on the relevance of such values and their hold on their lives.

Gibran did not seek to be a systematic philosopher. His insight came in revelatory flashes and he sought to flesh it out using equally rousing forms and forceful language to make reading his words a transformative experience. His prose works reveal an instinctive propensity for the inspiring aphorism (the short saying used in ancient wisdom literature), parable, short symbolic narrative and celebratory song. This is most evident in 1927's *Kalimat Gibran* (literally "The Words of Gibran") and the previous year's *Sand and Foam*. In *The Madman* (1918), *The Forerunner* (1920) and later *The Wanderer* (1932), he opted for the dramatizing technique of a speaking persona who lends a coherent narrative to insights Gibran neither wished to nor could expound on. Only in *The Prophet* and *Jesus, the Son of Man* was Gibran really able to achieve the harmony of voice and expression he had been working toward all his life. Gibran's art offers a more coherent expression of his vision. In the many recurring motifs, such as that of the trinity, in the paintings exploring different moods and existential states, in the various face studies, and especially the "Temple of Art" and in the "Centaur" series of paintings, Gibran systematically follows a single thought. Nature and the human body are one. Landscapes offer no vegetation, with the only natural phenomena being human forms, as in *The Mountain*, *The Rock* or *The Waterfall*. In this way, he depicts nature and mankind alike longing for their higher forms.

Detail from *The Rock*, 1916, Wash drawing, 11 x 8¾ inches (21 x 28 cm) Gibran Museum, Bisharri, Lebanon

THE ANTHOLOGY

Most of Kahlil Gibran's works are still in print, though except for Gibran devotees, readers tend to gravitate toward *The Prophet*. Indeed, it is the consummate expression of his life's achievements and powers of expression. While there have been numerous editions of *The Prophet* and a few other works, very few anthologies represent the full range of Gibran's prose and poetic works. Neither have there been authorized editions of his writing or art. The most recent anthology of his writing is Everyman's Library's *Kahlil Gibran, The Collected Works* (2007), which includes all Gibran's English work and a few, but not all, of his Arabic books and collections. The older three volumes of *A Treasury of Kahlil Gibran* offer translations of many of the Arabic pieces, but these need updating. There are numerous collections by different translators with a great deal of overlap, and translators tend to cull freely from the original volumes, changing or inventing titles without offering organizing principles for the selections.

I have chosen the pieces in this anthology from Gibran's entire English and Arabic œuvre, for the first time. Longer narrative or biographical pieces have not been anthologized, while aphorisms stand in their entirety, giving the reader the freedom to experience what they point to more intimately. The pieces of writing are grouped thematically in clusters. Rather than being arranged chronologically according to the order of their composition or appearance in print, they are organized according to the perceived central thought in each theme. I have been guided in this thematic arrangement by biographical themes; social, intellectual and philosophical themes; spiritual themes; Gibran's creative imagination and the power of the image; and by his transformation of biographical and historical details into visions of human potential. Each thematic cluster is accompanied by a biographical and critical commentary on the predominant ideas and values in the work.

Despite the wealth of biographies and critical studies of Gibran's work, his paintings and drawings have received relatively little attention and have never been systematically presented. No book yet presents and documents—let alone analyzes—the development of his artistic skill and vision. This has been the most lacking area of Gibran studies and still awaits serious and crucial work: chasing pieces in different museum and private collections, arranging and documenting them, and offering a serious art-historical study of this aspect of Gibran's vision. This volume provides, again for the first time, a representative range of Gibran's artistic offerings in different media. The paintings, drawings and portraits, selected from a lifetime of work, are arranged thematically to complement the text in the hope that the reader will enjoy a more holistic experience of Gibran's creative voice in image and in word.

Gibran strove throughout his life to perfect the expression of his vision and articulate the silent depths that resist expression. I hope the text in this volume points to that silence, the suggestion of transcendence and the vastness of the sources that inspired him. The chapters of this book are divided to reflect phases in Gibran's artistic and personal development, arranged in an ascending movement to culminate in a chapter on *The Prophet*. This ascending motion is guided by Gibran's phases of self-development: early intimations of Gibran as poet and artist make way for his visions of love, beauty, nature and the human condition, and then to articulations of exemplary human figures, reaching a peak with the Prophet. We might think of these phases or moments of revelation illuminating the life story of Gibran as a kind of "psychography." They help us to ask the questions: How can I live today as if my life were a gift from a possible future? And how can I respond to the summons of a potential I have sought out and which lies within me? To be modern is not only to attempt an answer but also to experience life as an expression of the act of answering. This is the message of Gibran, the modern self-begetter, who wished to beget a new offspring from his art and writings.

When assessing his words, artwork and philosophy, we must acknowledge that his genius is of this world, of "that which is between birth and death." There was no metaphysical system underpinning his work; rather, he presented glimpses of what was "shown" to him so that we might "look at the invisible" and understand how to transform the here and now in the name of the future. Kahlil Gibran did not write with academics or critics in mind, but wished first to express his innermost soul and by doing so touch the soul of every man and woman.

Detail from *Silence*, 1922, Watercolor, 22½ x 28¼ inches (72 x 57 cm) Gibran Museum, Bisharri, Lebanon

## CHAPTER 1

The ARTIST
and
the POET

Detail from *Self-Portrait*, 1908, Charcoal, 12½ x 17 inches (31.5 x 43 cm),
Gibran Museum, Bisharri, Lebanon

The Poet

THE POET in exile in this extract is also Kahlil Gibran's Madman, Forerunner, Wanderer and Prophet—the recurring characters who appear in his writing and art. All of them represent human possibility; all are creators, solitary visionaries and social rebels. These different namesakes for the poetic voice brought coherence to Gibran's visions and to his insight into many aspects of human life. Gibran referred to the possibility of his own potential variously as "the great power" in him, his "best self" or "greater self." And toward the end of his life, Gibran often referred to a higher being which wished to express itself through him; this became "the word" he desperately wished to articulate in his art and writings before his death. The aura surrounding Gibran's personality, enhanced by the enigma of his artistic works and the mysterious visions they expressed, attracted Boston's Bohemian and artistic circles of the 1890s, as did the mystique of the Orient. Bostonian poet Josephine Preston Peabody was the first to nurture Gibran's poetic talent and prophetic persona. In her attempt to understand the young Gibran's appeal, she described him in her diary on 21 November 1902 as having "the inescapable identity of...an angel or messenger of God."

BEHOLD ME a stranger unto this world! A stranger and an exile; and in exile there is a cruel aloneness and a painful solitude, which ever fill me with thoughts of a magical homeland never before known to me, and populate my dreams with spectres of a faraway land with no yesterdays.

A stranger am I, in the midst of my own kinsmen. And should I chance to meet one of them, I whisper to myself, "Who is this? And how do I know him? What natural laws bind us together, and why should I draw near and sit with him?"

A stranger am I, even unto myself. And should I hear what my own tongue utters, my ears deny my own voice. I see my own deeper self laughing, weeping, bracing itself, frightened; and my own being wonders at my own being, my spirit quizzing my own spirit. Yet do I remain unknown, hidden, veiled as if in mist, ungraspable, muted in my silence.

A stranger am I, detached from my own body. Whenever I stand before a mirror I see in my face what remains inscrutable in my soul, and in my eyes what the depths cannot fathom.

I roam the streets of the city, whereupon I find myself followed by young men shouting, "There he is, the Blind One! Let us give him a walking stick that he may tread with." And I hurriedly flee from them. I stumble into a coterie of young virgins who grasp at the hems of my garments, intoning, "As deaf as rock is he! Let us fill his ears with tunes of longing and love," and I jolt forward, leaving them behind me. Then I encounter a band of men, who gather round me, crying, "He is as mute as the grave! Let us straighten his tongue," and, frightened, I run away. I meet a group of venerable elders, who point in my direction with trembling fingers, saying, "Gone mad is he, lost his senses in beholden spectacles of jin and ghouls!"

Behold me, a stranger unto this world!

An exile am I, everywhere. Have I not roamed the face of the earth, East and West? And yet found I not my birthplace, nor one who has known me or heard of who I am.

And upon the morning I wake, only to find myself the captive of a darkened cavern with serpents dangling from its ceilings and insects crawling on all sides. I seek the light outside, advanced by the shadow of my body—but the shadows of my soul march abreast of me—whereto I know not, scouting matters beyond my grasp and grasping that which I need not.

And upon eventide I return and repose on bedding made of Ostrich feathers and sharp thorns. Strange thoughts begin to assail me; bedeviled with desires I lie, at once beguiled, pained, delighted.

At midnight, and through the crevices of the cavern, there creeps upon me the myriad shadows of bygone ages and the extinguished spirits of forgotten nations. I stare them in the face and they stare back; I address them quizzically and, smiling, they answer me. But when I reach out to grasp them, they recede and diminish as does smoke blown in the air.

Behold me, a stranger unto this world!

Detail from *John the Beloved Disciple*, 1928, Charcoal, 8½ x 11 inches (28 x 21.5 cm),
Gibran Museum, Bisharri, Lebanon

A stranger am I, and there is not one in existence who can cipher one word in the language of my soul.

I wander in the destitute wilderness, and, behold, rivulets rush upstream from the depths of the valley to the heights of the mountain top! Barren trees begin to blossom, produce fruit and shed all leaves, all in a flash! The towering branches lower to the earth and turn into shimmering spotted vipers!

I behold birds in random flight, upward, downward, singing, shrieking and then stand still, unfold their wings and turn into bare women with wildly unfurled hair and outstretched necks! They stare at me from behind eyelids darkened with the kohl of desire; they smile at me with reddened lips, dipped in honey; they stretch out with soft white hands, perfumed with frankincense and myrrh, then in a sudden moment, they flutter and vanish from before my sight, like mist in the air, leaving behind them the echoes of their mocking laughter!

Behold me, a stranger unto this world!

A poet am I. I bring together in verse what life has scattered in prose, and I strew in lines of prose what life has rendered in verse. Wherefore I shall ever be the stranger, and an exile I shall remain until death snatches me away and whisks me back to my homeland.

From *The Tempests,* 1920 (trans. Ayman A. El-Desouky)

A Song

GIBRAN BEGAN HIS creative career by composing Arabic poems, and was ecstatic when he was declared College Poet toward the end of his studies in *Madrasat al-Hikma*, Beirut's famous School of Wisdom. Here, he studied Arabic language and literature during a brief return to Lebanon from 1898 to 1901. Arabic poetry has a long tradition of poet-prophets, such as the 10th-century Al-Mutanabbi, whom Gibran admired. However, Gibran's most fundamental influence on his Arab contemporaries was a shift in emphasis, away from poetry as art and toward poetry as an expression of the poet's soul. This was a radical move at a time when classical form and style had a firm hold. Through his poetry and prose Gibran celebrated the poet as a solitary creator and a radical, rebellious shaper of language and values. For Gibran, the poet possesses a vision that he alone can express; the poet sings and by singing he manifests realities. He is "an angel sent by the gods to teach man the ways of gods."

Most radically, Gibran believed that the poet had the power to break the poetic molds of the *qasida* (the classical form of Arabic prosody that predominated for more than fourteen centuries) and to blur the line between poetry and prose, a virtual heresy until the 20th century.

In the depths of my soul there rises a song that refuses the garb of words!
A song that chooses but the numinous, wordless, innermost recesses of my heart for a dwelling!
A song that will not flow with ink on a parchment, but films my emotions delicately, transparently, clinging to my tongue like moisture that will not flow.

Shall I force it out, even in sighs, but how?
And I fear so for it, and I would shield it even from the delicate minutia of the ether!
And to whom shall I sing it?
It has long been accustomed to the serene recesses of my soul,
And I fear so for it, even from the harsh conduits of hearing!

When you look into my eyes, you will see but the reflected traces of its receding shadows.
When you touch the tips of my fingers, you will feel but its soft distant tremors.

All that my hands wrought are but the traces of its harmonies, as the lake mirrors the brightness of the stars.
My tears betray it the way dewdrops reveal the secrets of the rose, as they vanish into the heat of the day.

A song budding forth only in quietude,
Receding before the clamor of voice,
Intoned only in dreams,
Yet hidden upon wakefulness.

Such is the Song of Love, O' people!
What Legendary Ishaaq[1] can sound its tunes?
Nay, what Masterful David can incant it?

It has a fragrance sweeter than wafting jasmine,
What throats can capture it?
Better shielded than the precious secret of virgins,
What strings can proclaim it?

Who can fuse the roar of the seas with the warbling song of the Lark?
Who will dare the union of the howling seas with the sighing babe?

What mortal will dare the Song of the Gods?

From *A Tear and a Smile,* 1914 (Ayman A. El-Desouky)
1 Ishaaq Al-Mawsili, a legendary Arab lute player, singer and musician
   (A.D. 767–850)

The Two Poems

EASTERN PHILOSOPHY and Islamic *sufi* or mystical traditions strongly influenced Gibran. They led him to forge complex modes of expression and to a distinctly lyrical style, which gave new impetus in his Arabic writing to poetic prose, the prose poem and the emergent art of the short story. In his English writing, Gibran revived the arts of the aphorism, parable, short tale and other forms of expression used in wisdom literature (see page 59). In both languages, Gibran used Romantic forms to help him articulate the prophetic sense of his destiny—as an intermediary between God and man. In this, he followed the American philosopher-poet Ralph Waldo Emerson, whose 1844 essay *The Poet* set out a vision of man whose sensibility was powerful and revealing. Gibran's vision also recalled the poet-prophet of the English Romantic poet Percy Bysshe Shelley, who "beholds intensely the present as it is" and "participates in the eternal, the infinite, and the one" (*The Defence of Poetry,* 1840). Gibran commented to his famous "She-Angel," life-long intimate friend and generous benefactress Mary Haskell, "The only way to work is to do everything with the best that is in you. With the deepest heart of the heart and with the Eyes that are the fountain of the tears," which Mary carefully recorded in her Journal on 20 August 1920.

MANY CENTURIES AGO, on a road to Athens, two poets met, and they were glad to see one another.

And one poet asked the other saying, "What have you composed of late, and how goes it with your lyre?"

And the other poet answered and said with pride, "I have but now finished the greatest of my poems, perchance the greatest poem yet written in Greek. It is an invocation to Zeus the Supreme."

Then he took from beneath his cloak a parchment, saying, "Here, behold, I have it with me, and I would fain read it to you. Come, let us sit in the shade of that white cypress."

And the poet read his poem. And it was a long poem.

And the other poet said in kindliness, "This is a great poem. It will live through the ages, and in it you shall be glorified."

And the first poet said calmly, "And what have you been writing these late days?"

And the other answered, "I have written but little. Only eight lines in remembrance of a child playing in a garden." And he recited the lines.

The first poet said, "Not so bad; not so bad."

And they parted.

And now after two thousand years the eight lines of the one poet are read in every tongue, and are loved and cherished.

And though the other poem has indeed come down through the ages in libraries and in the cells of scholars, and though it is remembered, it is neither loved nor read.

From *The Wanderer*: *His Parables and Sayings*, 1932

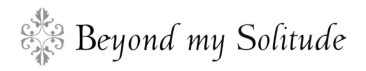

Beyond my Solitude

BEYOND MY SOLITUDE is another solitude, and to him who dwells therein my aloneness is a crowded marketplace and my silence a confusion of sounds.

Too young am I and too restless to seek that above-solitude. The voices of yonder valley still hold my ears, and its shadows bar my way and I cannot go.

Beyond these hills is a grove of enchantment and to him who dwells therein my peace is but a whirlwind and my enchantment an illusion.

Too young am I and too riotous to seek that sacred grove. The taste of blood is clinging in my mouth, and the bow and the arrows of my fathers yet linger in my hand and I cannot go.

Beyond this burdened self lives my freer self; and to him my dreams are a battle fought in twilight and my desires the rattling of bones.

Too young am I and too outraged to be my freer self.

And how shall I become my freer self unless I slay my burdened selves, or unless all men become free?

How shall my leaves fly singing upon the wind unless my roots shall wither in the dark?

How shall the eagle in me soar against the sun until my fledglings leave the nest which I with my own beak have built for them?

From *The Forerunner: His Parables and Poems*, 1920

"IF THERE IS anything in my work that draws people," Gibran confided in Mary Haskell, "it is probably that something that speaks to the aloneness in each one of us. I love to be alone...just let even a thumb's pressure be upon me to tame the wild something in me, and I feel it like a fetter." Gibran expressed these thoughts on an August afternoon in 1920, immediately after announcing to Mary that he had finished writing "On Crime and Punishment" in *The Prophet*. He was now channeling his aspirations for a freer, more confident and expressive self into the figure of the Prophet. Gibran grounded his lonely vision of the solitary creator and authentic individual in his understanding of humanity, which he regarded as an expression of one great spirit. Because we are all one body, he suggested delving deeper into one's self does not necessarily lead to isolation from others even if it frees one from external bonds. But complete personal freedom is only available to those who have aided others in their own struggle for liberation. As Gibran suggests in the final image of this extract, only once all his fledglings have learned to fly can the proud eagle soar alone, high in the skies of his own possibilities.

Kahlil Gibran in Late 19th-century Fashions of New York, c.1897,
Photographed by Fred Holland Day (1864–1933)

 Faces

"TO SEE A *'different'* face is to visit a new world," Gibran remarked to Mary Haskell on 2 April 1908. He was much taken by the shimmering mysteries of the human face, flashing with the inwardness and many selves for which he was eternally watchful. On 5 May, Mary recorded her impressions of Gibran's self-portrait, dedicated to her and featuring her face in the shadow: "His face changes like the shadows of leaves with every thought or feeling...It is a study in living beauty." One of Mary's first generous acts was to sponsor Gibran's trip to Paris between 1908 and 1910 where he could pursue his artistic talents more systematically. He enrolled at L'Académie Julian, a private academy boasting Henri Matisse, Pierre Bonnard and Fernand Léger among its alumni, and then at L'Ecole des Beaux-Arts. Gibran was taken on by sculptor Auguste Rodin. The "Temple of Art"— portraits of great artists and poets—is one of Gibran's remarkable artistic achievements. The gallery of greats include Abdul Baha (son of Baha'ullah, founder of the Bahá'í Faith), Giuseppe Garibaldi (grandson of the Italian hero), Claude Debussy and George Russell. Some subjects sat for him—Carl Jung, Rabindranath Tagore, W. B.Yeats—others Gibran drew from photographs or, in the case of Arab poets and philosophers, from his imagination.

I HAVE SEEN a face with a thousand countenances, and a face that was but a single countenance as if held in a mold.

I have seen a face whose sheen I could look through to the ugliness beneath, and a face whose sheen I had to lift to see how beautiful it was.

I have seen an old face much lined with nothing, and a smooth face in which all things were graven.

I know faces, because I look through the fabric my own eye weaves, and behold the reality beneath.

From *The Madman: His Parables and Poems*, 1918

Kahlil Gibran, c.1898, Photography by Fred Holland Day (1864–1933)

Heavy-Laden is my Soul

FROM EARLY ON and throughout his relationship with Josephine Peabody, Gibran was impressed by the Romantic concept of the artist as the unselfish giver. Josephine consciously cultivated this trait with him, though Gibran wished he could also offer her the financial security she aspired to. Gibran's family, just arrived in Boston in 1895, was barely making ends meet in the impoverished South End, a crowded, disease-ridden district. The family decided Gibran should attend school, while Kamila, his mother, worked to support them and enable Peter, Gibran's half-brother, to open a dry goods store. Sisters Mariana and Sultana worked as sales girls. Father Khalil remained in Bisharri in Lebanon, gradually fading from their lives. In Boston, Gibran Khalil Gibran took his Americanized name. It was there also that his innate talents were first recognized. He attended sketching classes in a charity organization, and came to the attention of Jessie Fremont Beale, an influential Bostonian who wrote the letter of introduction to Fred Holland Day that would change Gibran's life. A well-known artist and pioneering photographer, Day took the young Gibran under his wing as apprentice, protégé and one of his main subjects. Some of the best early photographs of Gibran and family were taken by Day, who introduced Gibran to Boston's artistic circles.

AND WHEN THE night was fully come, he took his steps to the graveside of his mother and sat beneath the cedar tree which grew above the place.

And there came the shadow of a great light upon the sky, and the Garden shone like a fair jewel upon the breast of earth.

And Almustafa cried out in the aloneness of his spirit, and he said:

"Heavy-laden is my soul with her own ripe fruit. Who is there would come and take and be satisfied? Is there not one who has fasted and who is kindly and generous in heart, to come and break his fast upon my first yieldings to the sun and thus ease me of the weight of mine own abundance?

"My soul is running over with the wine of the ages. Is there no thirsty one to come and drink?

"Behold, there was a man standing at the crossroads with hands stretched forth unto the passers-by, and his hands were filled with jewels. And he called upon the passersby, saying: 'Pity me, and take from me. In God's name, take out of my hands and console me.'

"But the passersby only looked upon him, and none took out of his hand.

"Would rather that he were a beggar stretching forth his hand to receive—ay, a shivering hand, and brought back empty to his bosom—than to stretch it forth full of rich gifts and find none to receive.

"And behold, there was also the gracious prince who raised up his silken tents between the mountain and the desert and bade his servants to burn fire, a sign to the stranger and the wanderer; and who sent forth his slaves

to watch the road that they might fetch a guest. But the roads and the paths of the desert were unyielding, and they found no one.

"Would rather that prince were a man of nowhere and nowhen, seeking food and shelter. Would that he were the wanderer with naught but his staff and an earthen vessel. For then at nightfall would he meet with his kind, and with the poets of nowhere and nowhen, and share their beggary and their remembrances and their dreaming.

"And behold, the daughter of the great king rose from sleep and put upon her silken raiment and her pearls and rubies, and she scattered musk upon her hair and dipped her fingers in amber. Then she descended from her tower to her garden, where the dew of night found her golden sandals.

"In the stillness of the night the daughter of the great king sought love in the garden, but in all the vast kingdom of her father there was none who was her lover.

"Would rather that she were the daughter of a ploughman, tending his sheep in a field, and returning to her father's house at eventide with the dust of the curving roads upon her feet, and the fragrance of the vineyards in the folds of her garment. And when the night is come, and the angel of the night is upon the world, she would steal her steps to the river-valley where her lover waits.

"Would that she were a nun in a cloister burning her heart for incense, that her heart may rise to the wind, and exhausting her spirit, a candle, for a light arising toward the greater light, together with all those who worship and those who love and are beloved.

"Would rather that she were a woman ancient of years, sitting in the sun and remembering who had shared her youth."

And the night waxed deep, and Almustafa was dark with the night, and his spirit was as a cloud unspent. And he cried again:

"Heavy-laden is my soul with her own ripe fruit;
Heavy-laden is my soul with her fruit.
Who now will come and eat and be fulfilled?
My soul is overflowing with her wine.
Who now will pour and drink and be cooled of the desert heat?
"Would that I were a tree flowerless and fruitless,
For the pain of abundance is more bitter than barrenness,
And the sorrow of the rich from whom no one will take
Is greater than the grief of the beggar to whom none would give.

"Would that I were a well, dry and parched, and men throwing stones
    into me;
For this were better and easier to be borne than to be a source of
    living water
When men pass by and will not drink.

"Would that I were a reed trodden under foot,
For that were better than to be a lyre of silvery strings
In a house whose lord has no fingers
And whose children are deaf."

From *The Garden of the Prophet,* 1933

On the Poet and the Artist

There is a space between man's imagination and man's
attainment that may only be traversed by his longing.

Should you care to write (and only the saints know why you
should) you must needs have knowledge and art and music—
the knowledge of the music of words, the art of being
artless, and the magic of loving your readers.

They dip their pens in our hearts and think they are inspired.

If I were to choose between the power of writing a poem and the
ecstasy of a poem unwritten, I would choose the ecstasy.
It is better poetry.
But you and all my neighbors agree that I always choose badly.

Poetry is not an opinion expressed. It is a song that rises from a
bleeding wound or a smiling mouth.

Words are timeless. You should utter them or write them with
a knowledge of their timelessness.

Auguste Rodin, 1910, Charcoal, Peter A. Juley & Son Collection, 8 x 10 inches (20.3 x 25.4 cm),
Smithsonian American Art Museum, Washington DC, USA

The Head of Orpheus Floating Down the River Hebrus to the Sea, c.1908–1914, Oil on canvas,
26 x 20 inches (51 x 66 cm), The Telfair Museum of Art, Savannah, Georgia

A poet is a dethroned king sitting among the ashes of his palace
trying to fashion an image out of the ashes.

Poetry is a deal of joy and pain and wonder, with a dash of
the dictionary.

In vain shall a poet seek the mother of the songs of his heart.

Once I said to a poet, "We shall not know your worth
until you die."
And he answered saying, "Yes, death is always the revealer.
And if indeed you would know my worth it is that I have
more in my heart than upon my tongue, and more in my
desire than in my hand."

Poetry is wisdom that enchants the heart.
Wisdom is poetry that sings in the mind.
If we could enchant man's heart and at the same time
sing in his mind,
Then in truth he would live in the shadow of God.

Inspiration will always sing; inspiration will never explain.

Thinking is always the stumbling stone to poetry.

A great singer is he who sings our silences.

There lies a green field between the scholar and the poet;
should the scholar cross it he becomes a wise man; should the
poet cross it, he becomes a prophet.

I long for eternity because there I shall meet my unwritten poems
and my unpainted pictures.

Art is a step from nature toward the Infinite.

A work of art is a mist carved into an image.

Every thought I have imprisoned in expression I must
free by my deeds.

From *Sand and Foam*, 1926

God Writing upon the Tables of the Covenant, c.1805, Pen, ink and watercolor over pencil and paper,
13½ x 16½ inches (41.9 x 34.1 mm), William Blake, National Gallery of Scotland, Edinburgh, Scotland.
"The most godly," is how Gibran saw Blake's vision, profoundly moved by his example as poet, artist
and visionary. Like Blake, Gibran wished to express his innermost thoughts, and in doing so, portray
a world that "can only be seen by the eye of the eye—never by the eye itself."

CHAPTER 2

LOVE
and
BEAUTY

Detail from *The Ethereal Being Sending a Message to Man*, 1920–1923,
Watercolor, 9½ x 13 inches (33 x 24 cm), Gibran Museum, Bisharri, Lebanon

Before the Throne of Beauty

AT THE HUB of Kahlil Gibran's worldview stands a holy triad: the creative and liberating forces of God, love and beauty. Deeply influenced by 19th-century Romanticism, Gibran believed beauty and truth to be synonymous, and in this extract they fuse in the form of a muse who counsels and consoles him. The same muse appeared in "The Queen of Fantasy" and "A Visit from Wisdom," both included in *A Tear and a Smile* (1914). With her "code of beauty and her credo of giving," she could only be Posy, Josephine Peabody, Gibran's first serious interlocutor and kindred spirit. The muse also showed up in the columns Gibran wrote for the New York-based Arabic newspaper *Al-Mohajer* (The Immigrant). Gibran approached its editor, Amin Gurayeb, when he visited Boston, offering him drawings for publication. But from the notebooks Gurayeb recognized that the young Gibran had an unusual poetic-prose style and asked him to write a column. It ran from 1906 under the title "Tears and Laughter" and marked the beginning of Gibran's writing career. Gibran would later contribute to the major New York-based Arabic newspapers and literary reviews: *Mir'at al-Gharb* (*The Mirror of the West*), *Al-Funun* (*The Arts*, 1913–1919) and *As-Sa'ih* (*The Traveler*, 1912–1931), all of which solidified his standing in the Arab world.

UPON A DAY, I decided to flee the intercourses of men and roam the wide valley, meandering about, following the running brooks or the warbling of birds. I paced here and there until I found a solitary spot, shielded by branches and protected from the intense gaze of the sun. Therein I sat, entertaining my aloneness and communing with my soul: forever thirsting, she considers all that is seen but a mirage, and all that is unseen, the promise of a soothing slake.

Sitting thus, freed from all that is material, my mind released into the expanses of the imagination, I suddenly turned and, lo and behold, there stood very near to me a young maiden! She stood as one of the *houris* of paradise, a nymph clad only in a branch of the vine; no other adornments save a crown of poppies binding her hair of gold. Noticing my bewildered looks, my eyes fixed on her, she said: "Fear not, I am the Daughter of the Forests!"

The sweetness of her voice revived me and brought back some composure. I asked in wonderment: "Do the likes of you inhabit such desolate wilderness, and among the wild beasts? Tell, I pray, who are you and whence have you come?" She replied as she sat on the grass: "I am the Symbol of Nature. I am the Virgin whom your forefathers worshipped, and for whom they erected temples and built shrines and altars in Baalbek and Aphaca and Byblos." "Those temples have long since been destroyed," I countered, "and the bones of my fathers long since merged with the land, with nothing left of their gods and their cults but a few yellowing pages buried in old tomes."

Upon which she answered: "Some gods live only for as long as their worshippers live, and die with them when they die. Other gods are primordial and eternal, ever the living divinity of the godhead. My divinity lies in the beauty you behold wheresoever you may turn your sight. A Beauty that is Nature itself. A Beauty that is the genesis of the shepherd's bliss among the hills, the farmer's in his fields, and that of the nomads as they roam from mountain to coast. Mine is the Beauty upon which the sage ascends to a truth that quickens."

My heart quickened to a rhythm beyond what my tongue could grasp, and yet I said: "Indeed, Beauty is an awesome, terrifying power!" With the smile of an open rose on her lips, and the secrets of life gleaming in her eyes, she answered: "You mortals always live in fear, dreading all, even yourselves! You fear the heavens, and they are but the abode of peace; you fear nature, and it is the haven of repose; you even fear The Lord God and ascribe to Him your meanness and wrath; and He is naught if not God the Lord of Love and Mercy!"

Upon the while, following a brevity of ecstatic repose, filled with soft, subtle visions, I asked: "What then is Beauty? People differ so in knowing and defining it, just as they diverge in their ways of glorifying and loving it." She answered: "Beauty is the hidden in you, which draws you to itself. Beauty is what, upon its beholding, you wish only to give not to receive, and when you encounter it, you feel as if arms have stretched forth from your depths to embrace it to your depths. Beauty is what tries the body, but to the spirit is a gift. It is the union of sorrow and joy. It is what you behold as if from behind a veil, and sense as the unknown, and hearken unto as if heeding silence. Beauty is a force that originates in the innermost sanctum of your soul, and ends in all that exceeds your wildest imagination!"

Upon this, the Daughter of the Forests drew nearer to me and laid her fragrant hand upon my eyelids. When she lifted her hand, I found but myself alone. I began my return, the while my soul intoned: "Indeed, Beauty is that which when you see it you wish but to give and not to receive!"

From *A Tear and a Smile,* 1914 (trans. Ayman A. El-Desouky)

# On Beauty

And a poet said, "Speak to us of Beauty."
  And he answered:

Where shall you seek beauty, and how shall you find her unless she herself be your way and your guide?

And how shall you speak of her except she be the weaver of your speech?

The aggrieved and the injured say, "Beauty is kind and gentle.
Like a young mother half-shy of her own glory she walks among us."
And the passionate say, "Nay, beauty is a thing of might and dread.
Like the tempest she shakes the earth beneath us and the sky above us."

The tired and the weary say, "Beauty is of soft whisperings.
She speaks in our spirit.
Her voice yields to our silences like a faint light that quivers in fear of the shadow."
But the restless say, "We have heard her shouting among the mountains,
And with her cries came the sound of hoofs, and the beating of wings and the roaring of lions."

At night the watchmen of the city say, "Beauty shall rise with the dawn from the east."
And at noontide the toilers and the wayfarers say, "We have seen her leaning over the earth from the windows of the sunset."

In winter say the snow-bound, "She shall come with the spring leaping upon the hills."
And in the summer heat the reapers say, "We have seen her dancing with the autumn leaves, and we saw a drift of snow in her hair."

All these things have you said of beauty.

Yet in truth you spoke not of her but of needs unsatisfied,

And beauty is not a need but an ecstasy.

It is not a mouth thirsting nor an empty hand stretched forth,

But rather a heart enflamed and a soul enchanted.

It is not the image you would see nor the song you would hear,

But rather an image you see though you close your eyes and a song you hear though you shut your ears.

It is not the sap within the furrowed bark, nor a wing attached to a claw,

But rather a garden for ever in bloom and a flock of angels for ever in flight.

People of Orphalese, beauty is life when life unveils her holy face.

But you are life and you are the veil.

Beauty is eternity gazing at itself in a mirror.

But you are eternity and you are the mirror.

From *The Prophet,* 1923

BEAUTY, FOR GIBRAN, is the force that unites the universe, motivating all emotions and relationships. It is balanced by truth, which governs our deeds. Pursuit of beauty and truth liberates us from external bonds —those imposed by society, religion or politics—Gibran advised in the early narratives of *Spirits Rebellious* from 1908, where the main characters illustrate struggles against social injustice, women's lack of rights, religious hypocrisy and the random nature of man-made laws. Similar messages lie behind the narratives collected in the 1912 book *The Broken Wings.* Gibran's views on beauty, love and women's rights set out in these early collections of Arabic writings won the heart and mind of May Ziadeh, his distant lover in Cairo, sparking a correspondence that is among the richest in modern Arabic literature. This began in 1912 when May first read Gibran's writing, and lasted until shortly before his death in 1931. May Ziadeh was born in Nazareth in 1886 to a Lebanese father from a village not far from Gibran's Bisharri and a Palestinian mother, but her family moved to Cairo in 1906. She eventually made a name for herself as a poet in Arabic and French, a literary critic and a feminist. Her Literary Salon in Cairo, held every Tuesday, became a social and scholarly institution for contemporary Arab intellectuals.

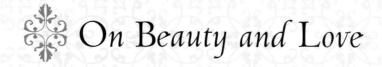

On Beauty and Love

If you sing of beauty though alone in the heart of the desert
you will have an audience.

When you reach the heart of life you shall find beauty in all
things, even in the eyes that are blind to beauty.

We live only to discover beauty. All else is a form of waiting.

There are only two elements here, beauty and truth; beauty in
the hearts of lovers, and truth in the arms of the tillers of the soil.

Great beauty captures me, but a beauty still greater frees me
even from itself.

Beauty shines brighter in the heart of him who longs for it than in
the eyes of him who sees it.

Love is the veil between lover and lover.

Love that does not renew itself every day becomes a habit
and in turn a slavery.

Lovers embrace that which is between them rather than each other.

Love and doubt have never been on speaking terms.

Love is a word of light, written by a hand of light,
upon a page of light.

From *Sand and Foam*, 1926

 # On Love

"LOVE HAS BECOME a halo whose beginning is its end, and whose end is its beginning. It surrounds every being and extends slowly to embrace all that shall be," Gibran wrote in 1912 in *The Broken Wings*. For Gibran, love of women—of his mother, sisters and female friends—was the light to his lamp and the flame of his creative soul. He wrote to May Ziadeh in 1928, "Women opened the windows of my eyes and the doors of my spirit." Before learning the pleasures of female companionship, first with Josephine Peabody and then with Mary Haskell, Micheline (otherwise known as Emilie Michel, a French teacher in the school founded by Mary Haskell) and many others, Gibran was well cared for by his mother Kamila and sisters Sultana and Mariana. But the course of true love never runs smoothly; indeed, Gibran saw pain as a necessary teacher. He first tasted the bitterness of love's defeat as a young man, during a brief return to Lebanon for his Arabic studies, with Salma Karame and Hala al-Dahir, both eventually betrothed to someone of higher social standing. The story formed the basis of *The Broken Wings*. After his return to Boston and an intense relationship, he was eventually snubbed by Josephine Peabody, who sought financial security in marriage to the affluent Lionel Marks.

THEN SAID ALMITRA, Speak to us of Love.

And he raised his head and looked upon the people, and there fell a stillness upon them. And with a great voice he said:

When love beckons to you, follow him,

Though his ways are hard and steep.

And when his wings enfold you yield to him,

Though the sword hidden among his pinions may wound you.

And when he speaks to you believe in him,

Though his voice may shatter your dreams as the north wind lays waste the garden.

For even as love crowns you so shall he crucify you. Even as he is for your growth so is he for your pruning.

Even as he ascends to your height and caresses your tenderest branches that quiver in the sun,

So shall he descend to your roots and shake them in their clinging to the earth.

Like sheaves of corn he gathers you unto himself.

He threshes you to make you naked.

He sifts you to free you from your husks.

He grinds you to whiteness.

He kneads you until you are pliant;

And then he assigns you to his sacred fire, that you may become sacred bread for God's sacred feast.

All these things shall love do unto you that you may know the secrets of your heart, and in that knowledge become a fragment of Life's heart.

But if in your fear you would seek only love's peace and love's pleasure,

Then it is better for you that you cover your nakedness and pass out of love's threshing-floor,

Into the seasonless world where you shall laugh, but not all of your laughter, and weep, but not all of your tears.

Love gives naught but itself and takes naught but from itself.

Love possesses not nor would it be possessed;

For love is sufficient unto love.

When you love you should not say, "God is in my heart," but rather, I am in the heart of God."

And think not you can direct the course of love, for love, if it finds you worthy, directs your course.

Love has no other desire but to fulfil itself.

But if you love and must needs have desires, let these be your desires:

To melt and be like a running brook that sings its melody to the night.

To know the pain of too much tenderness.

To be wounded by your own understanding of love;

And to bleed willingly and joyfully.

To wake at dawn with a winged heart and give thanks for another day of loving;

To rest at the noon hour and meditate love's ecstasy;

To return home at eventide with gratitude;

And then to sleep with a prayer for the beloved in your heart and a song of praise upon your lips.

From *The Prophet*, 1923

Mary Magdalen
On Meeting Jesus for the First Time

THIS IS ONE of the most touching and revealing portrayals of Mary Magdalen in Middle Eastern and Western literature. Mary's encounters with Jesus dramatized here depict Gibran's ideal of the redemptive power of love, which can only come about as one longs for the higher self. As his relationship with Mary Haskell deepened, Gibran began to emphasize the higher nature of the bond between them, which Mary recognized and recorded in her journals. Mary struggled with the deeper implications of this, eventually resigning herself to the fact that their relationship could neither become freely physical nor lead to marriage (see page 57). She hero-worshipped Gibran enough not to push their relationship too far, though she attempted to take it to a more personal level more than once. They maintained an intense correspondence and regularly visited between Boston and New York. Mary also supported Gibran financially and helped him with his first English drafts, more surreptitiously after deciding to marry Jacob Florance Minis and settle in Savannah, Georgia, in May 1926. Mary kept the promise she wrote of on 2 February 1915, "I am always with your coming self, Kahlil..."

Detail from *Love* (illustration for *The Prophet*), 1923, Watercolor, 8¼ x 11 inches (28 x 21 cm), Gibran Museum, Bisharri, Lebanon

IT WAS IN the month of June when I saw Him for the first time. He was walking in the wheatfield when I passed by with my handmaidens, and He was alone.

The rhythm of His steps was different from other men's, and the movement of His body was like naught I had seen before.

Men do not pace the earth in that manner. And even now I do not know whether He walked fast or slow.

My handmaidens pointed their fingers at Him and spoke in shy whispers to one another. And I stayed my steps for a moment, and raised my hand to hail Him. But He did not turn His face, and He did not look at me. And I hated Him. I was swept back into myself, and I was as cold as if I had been in a snowdrift. And I shivered.

That night I beheld Him in my dreaming; and they told me afterward that I screamed in my sleep and was restless upon my bed.

It was in the month of August that I saw Him again, through my window. He was sitting in the shadow of the cypress tree across my garden, and He was still as if He had been carved out of stone, like the statues in Antioch and other cities of the North Country.

And my slave, the Egyptian, came to me and said, "That man is here again. He is sitting there across your garden."

And I gazed at Him, and my soul quivered within me, for He was beautiful.

His body was single and each part seemed to love every other part.

Then I clothed myself with raiment of Damascus, and I left my house and walked toward Him.

Mary Haskell, 1908, Charcoal on laid paper, 12 × 17¾ inches (45 x 30.5 cm),
Telfair Museum of Art, Savannah, Georgia

Was it my aloneness, or was it His fragrance, that drew me to Him? Was it a hunger in my eyes that desired comeliness, or was it His beauty that sought the light of my eyes?

Even now I do not know.

I walked to Him with my scented garments and my golden sandals, the sandals the Roman captain had given me, even these sandals. And when I reached Him, I said, "Good-morrow to you."

And He said, "Good-morrow to you, Miriam."

And He looked at me, and His night-eyes saw me as no man had seen me. And suddenly I was as if naked, and I was shy.

Yet He had only said, "Good-morrow to you."

And then I said to Him, "Will you not come to my house?"

And He said, "Am I not already in your house?"

I did not know what He meant then, but I know now.

And I said, "Will you not have wine and bread with me?"

And He said, "Yes, Miriam, but not now."

Not now, not now, He said. And the voice of the sea was in those two words, and the voice of the wind and the trees. And when He said them unto me, life spoke to death.

For mind you, my friend, I was dead. I was a woman who had divorced her soul. I was living apart from this self which you now see. I belonged to all men, and to none. They called me harlot, and a woman possessed of seven devils. I was cursed, and I was envied.

But when His dawn-eyes looked into my eyes all the stars of my night faded away, and I became Miriam, only Miriam, a woman lost to the earth she had known, and finding herself in new places.

And now again I said to Him, "Come into my house and share bread and wine with me."

And He said, "Why do you bid me to be your guest?"

And I said, "I beg you to come into my house." And it was all that was sod in me, and all that was sky in me calling unto Him.

Then He looked at me, and the noontide of His eyes was upon me, and He said, "You have many lovers, and yet I alone love you. Other men love themselves in your nearness. I love you in your self. Other men see a beauty in you that shall fade away sooner than their own years. But I see in you a beauty that shall not fade away, and in the autumn of your days that beauty shall not be afraid to gaze at itself in the mirror, and it shall not be offended.

"I alone love the unseen in you."

Then He said in a low voice, "Go away now. If this cypress tree is yours and you would not have me sit in its shadow, I will walk my way."

And I cried to Him and I said, "Master, come to my house. I have incense to burn for you, and a silver basin for your feet. You are a stranger and yet not a stranger. I entreat you, come to my house."

Then He stood up and looked at me even as the seasons might look down upon the field, and He smiled. And He said again: "All men love you for themselves. I love you for yourself."

And then He walked away.

But no other man ever walked the way He walked. Was it a breath born in my garden that moved to the east? Or was it a storm that would shake all things to their foundations?

I knew not, but on that day the sunset of His eyes slew the dragon in me, and I became a woman, I became Miriam, Miriam of Mijdel.

From *Jesus, the Son of Man*, 1928

Portrait of May Ziadeh (from a photograph), 1920–1921, Charcoal,
8¾ x 11 inches (28 x 22 cm), Gibran Museum, Bisharri, Lebanon

Salome to a Woman Friend
A Desire Unfulfilled

IN A LETTER from Paris on 2 January 1909, Gibran confides to Mary Haskell, "I have loved a great deal—and I have always seen the beautiful: and between love and beauty I was and always shall be, a lost, hungry child of the Unknown." In Gibran's mind, the biblical figure of Salome became a symbol of action emerging out of passion. Love molds people in its fire, as Gibran wrote in *The Prophet*, and it is a master that must be obeyed. Love suspends society's conventions and even defies death. This message is apparent in Gibran's other writing, too, and is summarized in *The Life of Love*, his long poem from 1905 on the four seasons of love. Gibran was familiar both with biblical accounts of Salome, demanding the head of John the Baptist in return for dancing for King Herod, and with her depiction in high Renaissance art. The image of the severed head of John the Baptist is reminiscent of one of Gibran's early drawings of the severed head of Orpheus (see page 34), who sang out of love, mourning the loss of his beloved. For Gibran, both were key symbolic figures. Orpheus the singer poet and John the thundering prophet were emblems of his own dual self-perception, as Eastern and Western writer and as poet and prophet.

HE WAS LIKE poplars shimmering in the sun;
And like a lake among the lonely hills,
Shining in the sun;
And like snow upon the mountain heights,
White, white in the sun.

Yea, He was like unto all these,
And I loved Him.
Yet I feared His presence.
And my feet would not carry my burden of love
That I might girdle His feet with my arms.

I would have said to Him,
"I have slain your friend in an hour of passion.
Will you forgive me my sin?
And will you not in mercy release my youth
From its blind deed,
That it may walk in your light?"

I know He would have forgiven my dancing
For the saintly head of His friend.
I know He would have seen in me
An object of His own teaching.
For there was no valley of hunger He could not bridge,
And no desert of thirst He could not cross.
Yea, He was even as the poplars,
And as the lakes among the hills,
And like snow upon Lebanon.
And I would have cooled my lips in the folds of His
garment.

But He was far from me,
And I was ashamed.
And my mother held me back
When the desire to seek Him was upon me.

Whenever He passed by, my heart ached for his loveliness,
But my mother frowned at Him in contempt,
And would hasten me from the window
To my bedchamber.
And she would cry aloud saying,
"Who is He but another locust-eater from the desert?

What is He but a scoffer and a renegade,
A seditious riot-monger, who would rob us of sceptre and crown,
And bid the foxes and the jackals of His accursed land
Howl in our halls and sit upon our throne?
Go hide your face from this day,
And await the day when His head shall fall down,
But not upon your platter."
These things my mother said.
But my heart would not keep her words.
I loved Him in secret,
And my sleep was girdled with flames.

He is gone now.
And something that was in me is gone also.
Perhaps it was my youth
That would not tarry here,
Since the God of youth was slain.

From *Jesus, the Son of Man*, 1928

Nature Bending Over Man, Her Son, c.1913, Oil on canvas, 31½ x 25½ inches (65 x 80 cm),
Gibran Museum, Bisharri, Lebanon

Body and Soul

THIS PARABLE OF body-love and spirit-love illustrates some of the issues that have vexed Gibran's biographers and critics—and his lovers, too. His relationships with the key women in his life were sexually charged. Some clearly were sexually active (as with Micheline) and some had to be sublimated (as with Josephine Peabody). Gibran's longest lasting relationship with Mary Haskell quickly folded into complex redirected intimacies after a first awkward marriage proposal. Long, involved discussions followed about why they should not have intercourse. Gibran did, often evasively, insist both to Mary and May Ziadeh that their bond came from a higher source. He suggested that getting too involved, either physically or through marriage, would weaken this union, impeding their personal growth. Ultimately, we cannot explain why Gibran seemed to opt for abstraction and sublimation, though, by his own admission, it was a matter of "temperament"—he was reserved by nature and prone to privacy— rather than a code of virtue. Gibran once told Mary that the type of woman he found physically attractive was rare and that otherwise he felt repelled by the thought of physical intimacy. He would still insist, though, that the creator is the most highly charged and sexed being, and that he would channel this energy into his work.

A MAN AND a woman sat by a window that opened upon Spring. They sat close one unto the other. And the woman said, "I love you. You are handsome, and you are rich, and you are always well-attired."

And the man said, "I love you. You are a beautiful thought, a thing too apart to hold in the hand, and a song in my dreaming."

But the woman turned from him in anger, and she said, "Sir, please leave me now. I am not a thought, and I am not a thing that passes in your dreams. I am a woman. I would have you desire me, a wife, and the mother of unborn children."

And they parted.

And the man was saying in his heart, "Behold another dream is even now turned into mist."

And the woman was saying, "Well, what of a man who turns me into a mist and a dream?"

From *The Wanderer: His Parables and Sayings,* 1932

The Counsels of My Soul

MY SOUL COUNSELED me and instructed me in the love of all that others despise and the befriending of those whom they shun away.

My soul made me see that love is the gift of the beloved and not the virtue of the lover.

And unto the day my soul thus counseled, love had been for me but a fine thread stretching between two neighboring poles.

But now love has become a halo, without beginning and without end, encompassing all that is and ever waxing to encompass all that shall be.

My soul counseled and instructed me to discern beauty beyond the masks of shape, shade or complexion, and to stare into visibility the beauty of what others have declared an abomination.

And unto the day my soul thus counseled, beauty for me had been like unto dancing flames amid rising pillars of smoke, and that what burns after the vanishing smoke.

My soul counseled and instructed me to listen attentively to the sounds that are not born of tongues nor jangled in throats.

And unto the day my soul thus counseled, I had been thick and dull of hearing, able to discriminate only that which is hoarse and raucous.

But now I have begun to harken the stillness, listening to its depths as it chants the chants of ages and intones the canting rhythms of outer space, as it broadcasts the secrets of the unknown.

My soul counseled and instructed me to drink not from the wine of the press, nor from what is poured into cups or lifted by a hand or touched by lips.

And unto the day my soul thus counseled, I had thirsted but the thirst of a dim spark buried deep in a heap of ashes, easily quenched by a cupful of stream water or a sip from any old jar in the wine press.

But now my yearning has become my cup, my wine my own longing and my aloneness my elation.

But ever scorching shall my thirst remain, and it shall not be quenched.

And yet in this my unquenchable thirst shall be my eternal bliss.

My soul counseled and instructed me to reach out and touch what has not yet taken shape nor become body.

My soul made me to comprehend that what is given to the senses is but half the graspable,

That what we are able to grasp is only a fraction of what we wish to grasp.

And unto the day my soul thus counseled, I had contented myself with the heat when cold and with the chill when burning, and either one sufficed when indifferent.

But now my hitherto dormant extremities have quickened and turned into fine mist that penetrates all that appears in existence, seeking to become one with all that remains hidden.

From *Best Things and Masterpieces*, 1923
(trans. Ayman A. El-Desouky)

## CHAPTER 3

FAMILY, SOCIETY
and
FREEDOM

Detail from *Family Scene*, c.1913, Oil on canvas, 22 x 27 inches (68.7 x 56 cm),
Gibran Museum, Bisharri, Lebanon

On Marriage

KAHLIL GIBRAN never married, though he strongly believed in the union of spirits. He also thought that individuals joined in the sacred bond of love must retain their independence, maintaining that the personal and spiritual growth of each partner cannot take place unless their innermost core is free. "If I had a wife, and if I were painting or making poems," Barbara Young, Gibran's close associate and literary executor recalls him saying as he answered the queries of visitors, "I should simply forget her existence for days at a time. And you know very well no loving woman would put up with such a husband very long." Gibran feared that "the urge to express what is in him will absorb him too much for marriage," but was concerned as much for his female companion as his work. Gibran was keenly aware of women's right to be full, equal partners in a loving relationship, and treated the subject in some of his earliest writings: in 1908 in *Spirits Rebellious* and in *The Broken Wings* in 1912. The last lines in the section "On Marriage" from *The Prophet* have become among the most celebrated and quoted alternative texts for marriage vows in civil wedding ceremonies.

Then ALMITRA SPOKE again and said, And what of Marriage, master?

And he answered saying:

You were born together, and together you shall be forevermore.

You shall be together when white wings of death scatter your days.

Ay, you shall be together even in the silent memory of God.

But let there be spaces in your togetherness,

And let the winds of the heavens dance between you.

Love one another, but make not a bond of love:

Let it rather be a moving sea between the shores of your souls.

Fill each other's cup but drink not from one cup.

Give one another of your bread but eat not from the same loaf.

Sing and dance together and be joyous, but let each one of you be alone,

Even as the strings of a lute are alone though they quiver with the same music.

Give your hearts, but not into each other's keeping.

For only the hand of Life can contain your hearts.

And stand together, yet not too near together:

For the pillars of the temple stand apart,

And the oak tree and the cypress grow not in each other's shadow.

From *The Prophet*, 1923

# On Family

The song that lies silent in the heart of a mother sings upon
the lips of her child.

If there is such a thing as sin some of us commit it backward
following our forefathers' footsteps;
And some of us commit it forward by overruling our children.

Long were you a dream in your mother's sleep, and then
she woke to give you birth.

The germ of the race is in your mother's longing.

My father and mother desired a child and they begot me.
And I wanted a mother and a father and I begot night and the sea.

Once I saw the face of a woman, and I beheld all her
children not yet born.
And a woman looked upon my face and she knew all my
forefathers, dead before she was born.

From *Sand and Foam*, 1926

On Children

THIS EXTENDED metaphor of children and an archer has become one of Gibran's most enduring images. Gibran believed that in matters of love, both partners must be on a level footing, and if this is true of lovers, it is natural in the parent-child relationship, too. For Gibran, life is all there is and we are all—parents and children alike—equals among its many expressions. Children's "souls dwell in the house of tomorrow," he asserts, and parental yesterdays must not hinder the unfolding of these future possibilities. The statement that children "come through you but not from you" reveals Gibran's affiliations with Jungian psychology. He met Carl Jung several times in 1913 and executed an excellent portrait of him for his "Temple of Art" series (see page 27). In appreciation, Jung invited Gibran to visit him in Zurich for two weeks whenever he was in Europe. In 1957, Red Barber, a noted American sportscaster and a lay reader in the Episcopal Church, was presented with the millionth copy of *The Prophet*: "when a friend seems to be concerned about his children," Barber is said to have remarked, "I don't know anything better to do than give him a copy of *The Prophet* and ask him to read the section 'On Children' the first of every month."

Detail from *The Archer* (illustration for *The Prophet*), 1923, Watercolor, 8½ x 11 inches (27.8 x 21.5 cm), Gibran Museum, Bisharri, Lebanon

AND A WOMEN who held a babe against her bosom said, Speak to us of Children.

And he said:

Your children are not your children.

They are the sons and daughters of Life's longing for itself.

They come through you but not from you,

And though they are with you yet they belong not to you.

You may give them your love but not your thoughts.

For they have their own thoughts.

You may house their bodies but not their souls,

For their souls dwell in the house of tomorrow, which you cannot visit, not even in your dreams.

You may strive to be like them, but seek not to make them like you.

For life goes not backward nor tarries with yesterday.

You are the bows from which your children as living arrows are sent forth.

The archer sees the mark upon the path of the infinite, and He bends you with His might that His arrows may go swift and far.

Let your bending in the archer's hand be for gladness;

For even as He loves the arrow that flies, so He loves also the bow that is stable.

From *The Prophet*, 1923

On Work

CURRENT NOTIONS of work, and of measuring time by labor and leisure, are products of the Industrial Revolution and 19th-century ideological discourses. Gibran firmly cautioned against the encroachment of industrialization on human nature. "Something of vast value," he felt, "was being lost through the close and constant contact of men with machines, by way of the standardization that descended upon this country like a plague." Work, for Gibran, had pre-modern theological connotations; he regarded it an expression of life force. In order for work to be life-enhancing, or the essence of "proud submission toward the infinite," Gibran believed it must be in tune with both nature and human nature. He confided in Mary Haskell on 5 May 1922, "We are expressions of earth and of life—not separate individuals only." Gibran had a strict work routine himself, working for six hours a day, after which he would read and write letters or visit the library. Gibran always wished he could provide for his family, but insisted that he could only do so through his work and life-calling. So he was proud when, around 1918, he finally began to see some success, with the publication of *The Madman*, invitations to lecture between Boston and New York and to contribute to literary reviews and newspapers, and the sale of some paintings.

THEN A PLOUGHMAN said, Speak to us of Work.

And he answered, saying:

You work that you may keep pace with the earth and the soul of the earth.

For to be idle is to become a stranger unto the seasons, and to step out of life's procession, that marches in majesty and proud submission toward the infinite.

When you work you are a flute through whose heart the whispering of the hours turns to music.

Which of you would be a reed, dumb and silent, when all else sings together in unison?

Always you have been told that work is a curse and labor a misfortune.

But I say to you that when you work you fulfil a part of earth's furthest dream, assigned to you when that dream was born,

And in keeping yourself with labor you are in truth loving life,

And to love life through labor is to be intimate with life's inmost secret.

But if you in your pain call birth an affliction and the support of the flesh a curse written upon your brow, then I answer that naught but the sweat of your brow shall wash away that which is written.

You have been told also life is darkness, and in your weariness you echo what was said by the weary.

And I say that life is indeed darkness save when
there is urge,

    And all urge is blind save when there is knowledge,

    And all knowledge is vain save when there is work,

    And all work is empty save when there is love;

    And when you work with love you bind yourself to
yourself, and to one another, and to God.

    And what is it to work with love?

    It is to weave the cloth with threads drawn from your
heart, even as if your beloved were to wear that cloth.

    It is to build a house with affection, even as if your
beloved were to dwell in that house.

    It is to sow seeds with tenderness and reap the
harvest with joy, even as if your beloved were to eat
the fruit.

    It is to charge all things you fashion with a breath of
your own spirit,

    And to know that all the blessed dead are standing
about you and watching.

    Often have I heard you say, as if speaking in sleep,
"He who works in marble, and finds the shape of his
own soul in the stone, is a nobler than he who ploughs
the soil.

    And he who seizes the rainbow to lay it on a cloth in
the likeness of man, is more than he who makes the
sandals for our feet."

    But I say, not in sleep but in the over-wakefulness of
noontide, that the wind speaks not more sweetly to the
giant oaks than to the least of all the blades of grass;

And he alone is great who turns the voice of the wind into a song made sweeter by his own loving.

Work is love made visible.

And if you cannot work with love but only with distaste, it is better that you should leave your work and sit at the gate of the temple and take alms of those who work with joy.

For if you bake bread with indifference, you bake a bitter bread that feeds but half man's hunger.

And if you grudge the crushing of the grapes, your grudge distils a poison in the wine.

And if you sing though as angels, and love not the singing, you muffle man's ears to the voices of the day and the voices of the night.

From *The Prophet,* 1923

The Universal Mother Attracting Two Transcending Spirits, 1920–1923, Watercolor, 8¾ x 11 inches (27.8 x 22 cm), Gibran Museum, Bisharri, Lebanon

On Giving

THOUGH AS A young man, Gibran was influenced by the Romantic notion of the poet as an unselfish giver (see page 29), later in his career he profoundly reconceived his notion of giving, this time in terms of Christian and Muslim ideals. He believed that one should give what one loves most—one's self—and that everything in life should be offered and received as a gift. None of us, he stated, whether givers or recipients, can possess anything, from objects to other people. Whenever Gibran was beset with anxieties, over financial difficulties for example, he could confide in Mary Haskell, who shared his values. She came from an affluent South Carolinian family, inheriting from her father (the vice-president of a Columbia bank when she first met Gibran), not only wealth but her strength of character and sense of justice. "Things come to us from God, not from people," Mary wrote to Gibran on 29 November 1913, "but only *through* people; or from that in people which is beyond their limited humanity, from their god-self, *through* their limited human self." The theme of giving and receiving is one of the central motifs not only of Gibran's work but of his life and relationships, finding fullest expression toward the end of his life.

THEN SAID A rich man, Speak to us of Giving.
And he answered:

You give but little when you give of your possessions.

It is when you give of yourself that you truly give.

For what are your possessions but things you keep and guard for fear you may need them tomorrow?

And tomorrow, what shall tomorrow bring to the overprudent dog burying bones in the trackless sand as he follows the pilgrims to the holy city?

And what is fear of need but need itself?

Is not dread of thirst when your well is full, the thirst that is unquenchable?

There are those who give little of the much which they have—and they give it for recognition and their hidden desire makes their gifts unwholesome.

And there are those who have little and give it all.

These are the believers in life and the bounty of life, and their coffer is never empty.

There are those who give with joy, and that joy is their reward.

And there are those who give with pain, and that pain is their baptism.

And there are those who give and know not pain in giving, nor do they seek joy, nor give with mindfulness of virtue;

They give as in yonder valley the myrtle breathes its fragrance into space.

Though the hands of such as these God speaks, and from behind their eyes He smiles upon the earth.

It is well to give when asked, but it is better to give unasked, through understanding;

And to the openhanded the search for one who shall receive is joy greater than giving.

And is there aught you would withhold?

All you have shall some day be given;

Therefore give now, that the season of giving may be yours and not your inheritors'.

You often say, "I would give, but only to the deserving."

The trees in your orchard say not so, nor the flocks in your pasture.

They give that they may live, for to withhold is to perish.

Surely he who is worthy to receive his days and his nights, is worthy of all else from you.

And he who has deserved to drink from the ocean of life deserves to fill his cup from your little stream.

And what desert greater shall there be, than that which lies in the courage and the confidence, nay the charity, of receiving?

And who are you that men should rend their bosom and unveil their pride, that you may see their worth naked and their pride unabashed?

See first that you yourself deserve to be a giver, and an instrument of giving.

For in truth it is life that gives unto life—while you, who deem yourself a giver, are but a witness.

And you receivers—and you are all receivers—assume no weight of gratitude, lest you lay a yoke upon yourself and upon him who gives.

Rather rise together with the giver on his gifts as on wings;

For to be overmindful of your debt, is to doubt his generosity who has the frechearted earth for mother, and God for father.

From *The Prophet,* 1923

On Crime and Punishment

IN "THE CRY OF the Graves," included in *Spirits Rebellious* from 1908, Gibran presented parables that invite the reader to reconsider the injustice inherent in man-made laws and in society's measures of crime and methods of punishment. By examining the complexities of personal and social circumstance, Gibran unsettles everything that passes for positive law and clear judgment. He has the story's narrator ask poignantly, "Who are those who hanged the thief in the tree? Are they angels descended from heaven, or men looting and usurping? Who cut off the murderer's head? Are they divine prophets, or soldiers shedding blood wherever they go?" Gibran believed that though as individuals we are separate, we are all expressions of life, earth and heaven—and so all of us are implicated when one of us commits a misdeed, regardless of the harm done. His sense of justice rests ultimately on the value and sanctity of life, which can only be judged by its creator. Gibran's stance is an elaboration on Jesus's words to the angry crowd about to stone an adulterous woman, "He who is without sin among you, let him first cast a stone at her." (John 8:7). Man-made laws are borne of injustice, and the righteous in society must bear part of the blame.

THEN ONE OF the judges of the city stood forth and said, Speak to us of Crime and Punishment.

And he answered, saying:

It is when your spirit goes wandering upon the wind,

That you, alone and unguarded, commit a wrong unto others and therefore unto yourself.

And for that wrong committed must you knock and wait a while unheeded at the gate of the blessed.

Like the ocean is your god-self;

It remains for ever undefiled.

And like the ether it lifts but the winged.

Even like the sun is your god-self;

It knows not the ways of the mole nor seeks it the holes of the serpent.

But your god-self dwell alone in your being.

Much in you is still man, and much in you is not yet man,

But a shapeless pigmy that walks asleep in the mist searching for its own awakening.

And of the man in you would I now speak.

For it is he and not your god-self nor the pigmy in the mist, that knows crime and the punishment of crime.

Oftentimes have I heard you speak of one who commits a wrong as though he were not one of you, but a stranger unto you and an intruder upon your world.

But I say that even as the holy and the righteous cannot rise beyond the highest which is in each one of you,

So the wicked and the weak cannot fall lower than

the lowest which is in you also.

And as a single leaf turns not yellow but with the silent knowledge of the whole tree,

So the wrongdoer cannot do wrong without the hidden will of you all.

Like a procession you walk together toward your god-self.

You are the way and the wayfarers.

And when one of you falls down he falls for those behind him, a caution against the stumbling stone.

Ay, and he falls for those ahead of him, who though faster and surer of foot, yet removed not the stumbling stone.

And this also, though the word lie heavy upon your hearts:

The murdered is not unaccountable for his own murder,

And the robbed is not blameless in being robbed.

The righteous is not innocent of the deeds of the wicked,

And the white-handed is not clean in the doings of the felon.

Yea, the guilty is oftentimes the victim of the injured,

And still more often the condemned is the burden-bearer for the guiltless and unblamed.

You cannot separate the just from the unjust and the good from the wicked;

For they stand together before the face of the sun even as the black thread and the white are woven together.

And when the black thread breaks, the weaver shall look into the whole cloth, and he shall examine the loom also.

If any of you would bring to judgment the unfaithful wife,

Let him also weight the heart of her husband in scales, and measure his soul with measurements.

And let him who would lash the offender look unto the spirit of the offended.

And if any of you would punish in the name of righteousness and lay the axe unto the evil tree, let him see to its roots;

And verily he will find the roots of the good and the bad, the fruitful and the fruitless, all entwined together in the silent heart of the earth.

And you judges who would be just,

What judgment pronounce you upon him who though honest in the flesh yet is a thief in spirit?

What penalty lay you upon him who slays in the flesh yet is himself slain in the spirit?

And how prosecute you him who in action is a deceiver and an oppressor,

Yet who also is aggrieved and outraged?

And how shall you punish those whose remorse is already greater than their misdeeds?

Is not remorse the justice which is administered by that very law which you would fain serve?

Yet you cannot lay remorse upon the innocent nor lift it from the heart of the guilty.

Unbidden shall it call in the night, that men may wake and gaze upon themselves.

And you who would understand justice, how shall you unless you look upon all deeds in the fullness of light?

Only then shall you know that the erect and the fallen are but one man standing in twilight between the night of his pigmy-self and the day of his god-self,

And that the cornerstone of the temple is not higher than the lowest stone in its foundation.

From *The Prophet,* 1923

Mother and Child, Pre-1914, Oil on canvas, 18 x 26¾ inches (68 x 45.7 cm), Gibran Museum, Bisharri, Lebanon

On Freedom

And an orator said, Speak to us of Freedom.
And he answered:

At the city gate and by your fireside I have seen you prostrate yourself and worship your own freedom,

Even as slaves humble themselves before a tyrant and praise him though he slays them.

Ay, in the grove of the temple and in the shadow of the citadel I have seen the freest among you wear their freedom as a yoke and a handcuff.

And my heart bled within me; for you can only be free when even the desire of seeking freedom becomes a harness to you, and when you cease to speak of freedom as a goal and a fulfilment.

You shall be free indeed when your days are not without a care nor your nights without a want and a grief,

But rather when these things girdle your life and yet you rise above them naked and unbound.

And how shall you rise beyond your days and nights unless you break the chains which you at the dawn of your understanding have fastened around your noon hour?

In truth that which you call freedom is the strongest of these chains, though its links glitter in the sun and dazzle your eyes.

And what is it but fragments of your own self you would discard that you may become free?

If it is an unjust law you would abolish, that law was written with your own hand upon your own forehead.

You cannot erase it by burning your law books nor by washing the foreheads of your judges, though you pour the sea upon them.

And if it is a despot you would dethrone, see first that his throne erected within you is destroyed.

FREEDOM IS NOT found in the absence of all that restrains man's nature, said Gibran; rather, we achieve freedom by embracing and overcoming those human fetters and working toward higher qualities. In his well-known Arabic long poem *The Processions* (1919), Gibran included a section on freedom and prepared a series of drawings. He showed them to Mikhail Naimy, one of his first biographers and closest Lebanese literary comrades. Naimy commented on the drawing on Freedom, which he felt to be "a kind of spiritual self-portrait." The powerfully built man with wings in this painting is typical of Gibran's Blakean figures. The English poet-artist William Blake was one of Gibran's earliest influences. Like Blake, he sought to express his innermost struggles in his allegorical drawings of man and nature, and through them to awaken a similar quest in others. Gibran's artistic debut came in 1903 in an exhibition at Wellesley College in Massachusetts, arranged by Josephine Peabody. A year later she helped mount his pieces in an exhibition in Fred Holland Day's studio. Unfortunately, the studio was destroyed by fire, another setback for the young Gibran, who had recently lost his sister, half-brother and mother. However, it was at this exhibition that the auspicious first meeting took place between Gibran and Mary Haskell.

For how can a tyrant rule the free and the proud, but for a tyranny in their own freedom and a shame in their own pride?

And if it is a care you would cast off, that care has been chosen by you rather than imposed upon you.

And if it is a fear you would dispel, the seat of that fear is in your heart and not in the hand of the feared.

Verily all things move within your being in constant half embrace, the desired and the dreaded, the repugnant and the cherished, the pursued and that which you would escape.

These things move within you as lights and shadows in pairs that cling.

And when the shadow fades and is no more, the light that lingers becomes a shadow to another light.

And thus your freedom when it loses its fetters becomes itself the fetter of a greater freedom.

From *The Prophet,* 1923

On Society and Freedom

How can I lose faith in the justice of life, when the dreams of those who sleep upon feathers are not more beautiful than the dreams of those who sleep upon the earth?

We are all beggars at the gate of the temple, and each one of us receives his share of the bounty of the King when he enters the temple, and when he goes out.
But we are all jealous of one another, which is another way of belittling the King.

You cannot consume beyond your appetite. The other half of the loaf belongs to the other person, and there should remain a little bread for the chance guest.

If it were not for your guests all houses would be graves.

I stopped my guest on the threshold and said, "Nay, wipe not your feet as you enter, but as you go out."

The Family of the Artist, 1914, Oil on canvas, 36 x 25½ inches (65.5 × 91.5 cm),
Gibran Museum, Bisharri, Lebanon

Generosity is not in giving me that which I need more than you do, but it is in giving me that which you need more than I do.

You are indeed charitable when you give, and while giving, turn your face away so that you may not see the shyness of the receiver.

The difference between the richest man and the poorest is but a day of hunger and an hour of thirst.

You may judge others only according to your knowledge of yourself.
Tell me now, who among us is guilty and who is unguilty?

You cannot judge any man beyond your knowledge of him, and how small is your knowledge.

The truly just is he who feels half guilty of your misdeeds.

Only an idiot and a genius break man-made laws;
and they are the nearest to the heart of God.

The only one who has been unjust to me is the one to whose
brother I have been unjust.

Oftentimes I have hated in self-defense; but if I were stronger
I would not have used such a weapon.

How stupid is he who would patch the hatred in his eyes
with the smile of his lips.

How mean am I when life gives me gold and I give you silver,
and yet I deem myself generous.

Strange that we all defend our wrongs with more vigor
than we do our rights.

From *Sand and Foam*, 1926

Pity the Nation!

GIBRAN BELIEVED in a just society. He was ever suspicious of the restrictions imposed on citizens by narrow notions of nations and nationalism, and he elaborated on this theme in "You have Your Lebanon and I have Mine," a speech later included in *Al-Bada'i' wa al-Tara'if* (*Best Things and Masterpieces*, 1923). Gibran felt that he was both Lebanese and American—and wholly neither. For him, the individual came first and national identity second, and he distrusted all forms of government. "Government is an agreement between you and myself. You and myself are often wrong," he wrote in *Sand and Foam* (1926). Here, he also confirmed his faith in the individual, "If you would rise but a cubit above race and country and self you would indeed become godlike." But when it came to the struggle for freedom, Gibran saw war as a natural state of affairs, through which nations could renew their freedom and their founding principles. On 14 October 1914, with World War I raging, Gibran wrote to Mary Haskell, "We are living this war; you and I. All those who live the collective life of this world—are struggling, like you and me, with the nations of Europe. And it is a noble struggle."

AND ALMUSTAFA CAME and found the Garden of his mother and his father, and he entered in, and closed the gate that no man might come after him.

And for forty days and forty nights he dwelt alone in that house and that Garden, and none came, not even unto the gate, for it was closed, and all the people knew that he would be alone.

And when the forty days and nights were ended, Almustafa opened the gate that they might come in.

And there came nine men to be with him in the Garden; three mariners from his own ship; three who had served in the Temple; and three who had been his comrades in play when they were but children together. And these were his disciples.

And on a morning his disciples sat around him, and there were distances and remembrances in his eyes. And that disciple who was called Hafiz said unto him: "Master, tell us of the city of Orphalese, and of that land wherein you tarried those twelve years."

And Almustafa was silent, and he looked away toward the hills and toward the vast ether, and there was a battle in his silence.

Then he said: "My friends and my road-fellows, pity the nation that is full of beliefs and empty of religion.

"Pity the nation that wears a cloth it does not weave, eats a bread it does not harvest, and drinks a wine that flows not from its own winepress.

"Pity the nation that acclaims the bully as hero, and that deems the glittering conqueror bountiful.

"Pity the nation that despises a passion in its dream, yet submits in its awakening.

"Pity the nation that raises not its voice save when it walks in a funeral, boasts not except among its ruins, and will rebel not save when its neck is laid between the sword and the block.

"Pity the nation whose statesman is a fox, whose philosopher is a juggler, and whose art is the art of patching and mimicking.

"Pity the nation that welcomes its new ruler with trumpetings, and farewells him with hootings, only to welcome another with trumpetings again.

"Pity the nation whose sages are dumb with years and whose strong men are yet in the cradle.

"Pity the nation divided into fragments, each fragment deeming itself a nation."

From *The Garden of the Prophet*, 1933

We Live Upon One Another

THE ONE INEXORABLE law in the Gibranian universe is the interdependence of all forms of life: between individuals, within nature and in moral, social and political justice. Though Gibran was outspoken in criticizing the burgeoning capitalism of the early 20th century, he was equally critical of socialism, which he felt appealed to the lowest common denominator and did not seek to bring out the best in all people. In New York Gibran commanded different voices. He became associated with socialists when invited onto the editorial board of the literary journal *The Seven Arts*, edited by poet James Oppenheim. At the same time, he was becoming active among the New York-based circles of radical Arab nationalists who were beginning to rally for independence from Turkish rule. During the years of World War I, Gibran fantasized about being a fighter and revolutionary. He resented not being invited along with his friends Najib Diab and Amin Rihani to represent the Arab immigrant community at the First Arab Congress in Paris, which was calling for Home Rule for the Arab territories. Gibran himself called for all-out revolution rather than political resolution, which he deemed futile, and he seems to have hatched plans with General Garibaldi, whose company he enjoyed while drawing his portrait for the "Temple of Art" series.

AND UPON A day as they sat in the long shadows of the white poplars, one spoke saying: "Master, I am afraid of time. It passes over us and robs us of our youth, and what does it give in return?"

And he answered and said: "Take up now a handful of good earth. Do you find in it a seed, and perhaps a worm? If your hand were spacious and enduring enough, the seed might become a forest, and the worm a flock of angels. And forget not that the years which turn seeds to forests, and worms to angels, belong to this *Now*, all of the years, this very *Now*.

"And what are the seasons of the years save your own thoughts changing? Spring is an awakening in your breast, and summer but a recognition of your own fruitfulness. Is not autumn the ancient in you singing a lullaby to that which is still a child in your being? And what, I ask you, is winter save sleep big with the dreams of all the other seasons."

And then Mannus, the inquisitive disciple, looked about him and he saw plants in flower cleaving unto the sycamore tree.

And he said: "Behold the parasites, Master. What say you of them? They are thieves with weary eyelids who steal the light from the steadfast children of the sun, and make fair of the sap that runneth into their branches and their leaves."

And he answered him saying: "My friend, we are all parasites. We who labor to turn the sod into pulsing life are not above those who receive life directly from the sod without knowing the sod.

"Shall a mother say to her child: 'I give you back to the forest, which is your greater mother, for you weary me, heart and hand'?

"Or shall the singer rebuke his own song, saying: 'Return now to the cave of echoes from whence you came, for your voice consumes my breath'?

"And shall the shepherd say to his yearling: 'I have no pasture whereunto I may lead you; therefore be cut off and become a sacrifice for this cause'?

"Nay, my friend, all these things are answered even before they are asked, and, like your dreams, are fulfilled ere you sleep.

"We live upon one another according to the law, ancient and timeless. Let us live thus in loving-kindness. We seek one another in our aloneness, and we walk the road when we have no hearth to sit beside.

"My friends and my brothers, the wider road is your fellow man.

"These plants that live upon the tree draw milk of the earth in the sweet stillness of night, and the earth in her tranquil dreaming sucks at the breast of the sun.

"And the sun, even as you and I and all there is, sits in equal honor at the banquet of the Prince whose door is always open and whose board is always spread.

"Mannus, my friend, all there is lives always upon all there is; and all there is lives in the faith, shoreless, upon the bounty of the Most High."

From *The Garden of the Prophet,* 1933

## CHAPTER 4

GOD, FAITH
and
RELIGION

Detail from *The Prayer* (illustration for *The Prophet*), 1923, Watercolor,
8¼ x 11 inches (28 x 21 cm), Gibran Museum, Bisharri, Lebanon

# On Prayer

THEN A PRIESTESS said, Speak to us of Prayer.
And he answered, saying:

You pray in your distress and in your need; would that you might pray also in the fullness of your joy and in your days of abundance.

For what is prayer but the expansion of yourself into the living ether?

And if it is for your comfort to pour your darkness into space, it is also for your delight to pour forth the dawning of your heart.

And if you cannot but weep when your soul summons you to prayer, she should spur you again and yet again, though weeping, until you shall come laughing.

When you pray you rise to meet in the air those who are praying at that very hour, and whom save in prayer you may not meet.

Therefore let your visit to that temple invisible be for naught but ecstasy and sweet communion.

For if you should enter the temple for no other purpose than asking you shall not receive:

And if you should enter into it to humble yourself you shall not be lifted:

Or even if you should enter into it to beg for the good of others you shall not be heard.

It is enough that you enter the temple invisible.

I cannot teach you how to pray in words.

God listens not to your words save when He Himself utters them through your lips.

And I cannot teach you the prayer of the seas and the forests and the mountains.

But you who are born of the mountains and the forests and the seas can find their prayer in your heart,

And if you but listen in the stillness of the night you shall hear them saying in silence,

"Our God, who art our winged self, it is thy will in us that willeth.

It is thy desire in us that desireth.

It is thy urge in us that would turn our nights, which are thine, into days which are thine also.

We cannot ask thee for aught, for thou knowest our needs before they are born in us:

Thou art our need; and in giving us more of thyself thou givest us all."

From *The Prophet,* 1923

KAHLIL GIBRAN'S RENDITION of the Lord's Prayer at the end of this extract sums up his answer to the ritualized prayers of institutionalized religion. He thought that such worded physical and visible prayers would lead to the hypocritical religious practices he abhorred. The "temple invisible" described here is clearly reminiscent of William Blake's "Universal Brotherhood of Eden" in *The Four Zoas,* composed around the turn of the 19th century. However, the doctrine of prayer in "ecstasy and sweet communion" also reveals the strong influence of Islamic and Jewish mysticism on Gibran. Evidence of this abounds in *The Prophet*: *wihdat al-wujud* or unity of existence, *al-Insan al-Kamil* or the Perfect Man, the divine source in man and nature, oneness of all religions, and the unity of life and death, good and evil, time and space. Gibran found echoes of these ideas in Ralph Waldo Emerson's 1841 essay "The Over-Soul," in the writings of the 18th-century scientist and philosopher Emanuel Swedenborg, in the work of contemporary spiritual thinkers J. Krishnamurti and G. I. Gurdjieff, and in the visions of the theosophists, disseminated by Madame Blavatsky's circles in Boston, New York and London. By the 1920s, Gibran was channeling these early influences into the positively inspiring figure of Almustafa in *The Prophet*.

Detail from *The Birth of God*, 1912–1916, Oil on cardboard,
14 x 20¼ inches (51.5 x 35.7 cm), Gibran Museum, Bisharri, Lebanon

God

"THIS PERCEPTION, beloved Mary, this new knowledge of God is with me night and day," Gibran wrote to Mary Haskell on 30 January 1916, two years after publication of *The Madman*. The "new knowledge" revealed to Gibran was that the essence of God is also the spirit of the earth and the soul of man. God is not simply the creator, Gibran stated, but the supreme "desirer," who first desired himself and then desired man and earth to become like him. Gibran described the way in which God came into existence, "rising like the mist from the seas and the mountains and plains," without knowing himself fully. But as he evolved through his will, power and desire, so man came into being, too. Gibran believed that everything in existence—including our souls and the spirit of the earth—rises toward God through the force of desire. He felt that this revelation would radically transform our understanding of the divine, our knowledge of ourselves, and our relationship with one another and the earth. Once we realize that God evolves and that we develop with him, we can seek God with consciousness and knowledge, rather than through institutions or theological formulae. Gibran's early painting "The Birth of God" is a faithful visualization of this intuition.

IN THE ANCIENT days, when the first quiver of speech came to my lips, I ascended the holy mountain and spoke unto God, saying, "Master, I am thy slave. Thy hidden will is my law and I shall obey thee for ever more."

But God made no answer, and like a mighty tempest passed away.

And after a thousand years I ascended the holy mountain and again spoke unto God, saying, "Creator, I am thy creation. Out of clay hast thou fashioned me and to thee I owe mine all."

And God made no answer, but like a thousand swift wings passed away.

And after a thousand years I climbed the holy mountain and spoke unto God again, saying, "Father, I am thy son. In pity and love thou hast given me birth, and through love and worship I shall inherit thy kingdom."

And God made no answer, and like the mist that veils the distant hills he passed away.

And after a thousand years I climbed the sacred mountain and again spoke unto God, saying, "My God, my aim and my fulfilment; I am thy yesterday and thou are my tomorrow. I am thy root in the earth and thou art my flower in the sky, and together we grow before the face of the sun."

Then God leaned over me, and in my ears whispered words of sweetness, and even as the sea that enfoldeth a brook that runneth down to her, he enfolded me.

And when I descended to the valleys and the plains God was there also.

From *The Madman: His Parables and Poems*, 1918

God and Many Gods

IN THE PARABLES of Jesus, Gibran found a powerful form of expression. He valued the way in which the parable speaks to everyday people while revealing the force of personality of the speaker: to grasp the meaning of the piece is at once to experience the person speaking. On 14 September 1920, Mary Haskell recorded a clear account of Gibran's view of God in her private journals: "There is an aloneness in every man. He can be helped to look at the invisible. It may take a long time to reach a consciousness of God. God can't be demonstrated. I never tried to prove his existence. The idea of God is different in every man, and one can never give another his own religion." He had also told her that the Maronite Church, the Lebanese Catholic Church, had considered excommunicating him after the publication of *Nymphs of the Valley* in 1906 on grounds of heresy. Back in 1908, Gibran had written to his cousin N'oula Gibran on 15 March, describing how he was beginning to be regarded as a heretic, but no record of excommunication has ever been found. On his deathbed, unable to be confessed or given communion by a Maronite priest in New York, Gibran's literary comrade Mikhail Naimy had to intercede to enable a church burial to take place back in Boston.

IN THE CITY of Kilafis a sophist stood on the steps of the Temple and preached many gods. And the people said in their hearts, "We know all this. Do they not live with us and follow us wherever we go?"

Not long after, another man stood in the market place and spoke unto the people and said, "There is no god." And many who heard him were glad of his tidings, for they were afraid of gods.

And upon another day there came a man of great eloquence, and he said, "There is but one God." And now the people were dismayed for in their hearts they feared the judgment of one God more than that of many gods.

That same season there came yet another man, and he said to the people, "There are three gods, and they dwell upon the wind as one, and they have a vast and gracious mother who is also their mate and their sister."

Then everyone was comforted, for they said in their secret, "Three gods in one must needs disagree over our failings, and besides, their gracious mother will surely be an advocate for us poor weaklings."

Yet even to this day there are those in the city of Kilafis who wrangle and argue with each other about many gods and no god, and one god and three gods in one, and a gracious mother of gods.

From *The Wanderer: His Parables and Sayings,* 1932

Detail from *Crucified on the Tower of Humanity and Religions*, 1918, Pencil, 8¼ x 11 inches (28 x 21 cm), Gibran Museum, Bisharri, Lebanon

❧ A God unto a God

"GOD DESIRES MAN and earth to become like Him, and a part of Him. God is growing through his desire, and man and earth, and all there is upon the earth, rise toward God by the power of desire," Gibran wrote to Mary Haskell from New York on 30 January 1916. Abstract metaphysics and the God of the clouds—removed, abstract, inscrutable and alien—never interested Gibran. He was fascinated in the God in man that has yet to grow out of man. A month later he wrote to Mary again, "When the soul reaches God it will be conscious that it is God, and that it is seeking more of itself in being in God, and that God too is growing and seeking and crystallizing." This is a hard path to follow, Gibran found. But despite illness and creative fatigue toward the end of his life, and the saddening suspicion that he had yet to tally with the image of his greater self, Gibran held strongly to his beliefs. *The Garden of the Prophet* appeared posthumously in 1933.

AND ON THE first day of the week when the sounds of the temple bells sought their ears, one spoke and said: "Master, we hear much talk of God hereabout. What say you of God, and who is He in very truth?"

And he stood before them like a young tree, fearless of wind or tempest, and he answered saying: "Think now, my comrades and beloved, of a heart that contains all your hearts, a love that encompasses all your loves, a spirit that envelops all your spirits, a voice enfolding all your voices, and a silence deeper than all your silences, and timeless.

"Seek now to perceive in your selffulness a beauty more enchanting than all things beautiful, a song more vast than the songs of the sea and the forest, a majesty seated upon the throne for which Orion is but a footstool, holding a sceptre in which the Pleiades are naught save the glimmer of dewdrops.

"You have sought always only food and shelter, a garment and a staff; seek now One who is neither an aim for your arrows nor a stony cave to shield you from the elements.

"And if my words are a rock and a riddle, then seek, none the less, that your hearts may be broken, and that your questionings may bring you unto the love and the wisdom of the Most High, whom men call God."

And they were silent, every one, and they were perplexed in their heart; and Almustafa was moved with compassion for them, and he gazed with tenderness upon them and said: "Let us speak no more now of God the Father. Let us speak rather of the gods, your neighbors, and of your brothers, the elements that move about your houses and your fields.

"You would rise in fancy unto the cloud, and you deem it height; and you would pass over the vast sea and claim it to be distance. But I say unto you that when you sow a seed in the earth, you reach a greater height; and when you hail the beauty of the morning to your neighbor, you cross a greater sea.

"Too often do you sing God, the Infinite, and yet in truth you hear not the song. Would that you might listen to the songbirds, and to the leaves that forsake the branch when the wind passes by, and forget not, my friends, that these sing only when they are separated from the branch!

"Again I bid you to speak not so freely of God, who is your All, but speak rather and understand one another, neighbor unto neighbor, a god unto a god.

"For what shall feed the fledgling in the nest if the mother bird flies skyward? And what anemone in the field shall be fulfilled unless it be husbanded by a bee from another anemone?

"It is only when you are lost in your smaller selves that you seek the sky which you call God. Would that you might find paths into your vast selves; would that you might be less idle and pave the roads!

"My mariners and my friends, it were wiser to speak less of God, whom we cannot understand, and more of each other, whom we may understand. Yet I would have you know that we are the breath and the fragrance of God. We are God, in leaf, in flower, and oftentimes in fruit."

From *The Garden of the Prophet,* 1933

Detail from *The Triangle*, 1918, (published in *Twenty Drawings*, 1919), Wash drawing,
8¾ x 9¾ inches (25 x 20 cm), Gibran Museum, Bisharri, Lebanon

Out of My Deeper Heart

THE FORERUNNER, initially named The Lonely One, is another of Gibran's fictive figures. He is the creator revealed as an outcast and rebel, free and strong enough to push not only at the boundaries of society's conventions but at the limitations of man's nature. The Forerunner—"he who calls himself echo to a voice yet unheard"— is able to see the future in the present and to seek it uninhibited by the views of those who still live in the past, imprisoned in obsolete traditions. Gibran fervently sought to realize his personal destiny through his writing and painting. "To you now, what you write and paint expresses mere fragments of your vision," Mary Haskell wrote to him on 16 November 1913. "But in time the whole vision will appear in it. For man will learn to see and hear and read. And your work is not only books and pictures. They are but bits of it. Your work is You, not less than you, not parts of you... Your silence will be read with your writings some day, your darkness will be part of the Light." These generous insights have become famous subsequently: they foretold the future after *The Prophet*, and stressed the silence, with which Gibran was obsessed. This, he felt, was the real promise behind his "worded knowledge."

OUT OF MY deeper heart a bird rose and flew skyward.

Higher and higher did it rise, yet larger and larger did it grow.

At first it was but like a swallow, then a lark, then an eagle, then as vast as a spring cloud and then it filled the starry heavens.

Out of my heart a bird flew skyward. And it waxed larger as it flew. Yet it left not my heart.

O my faith, my untamed knowledge, how shall I fly to your height and see with you man's larger self penciled upon the sky?

How shall I turn this sea within me into mist, and move with you in space immeasurable?

How can a prisoner within the temple behold its golden domes?

How shall the heart of a fruit be stretched to envelop the fruit also?

O my faith, I am in chains behind these bars of silver and ebony, and I cannot fly with you.

Yet out of my heart you rise skyward, and it is my heart that holds you, and I shall be content.

From *The Forerunner: His Parables and Poems,* 1920

On Religion

AND AN OLD PRIEST said, Speak to us of Religion.

And he said:

Have I spoken this day of aught else?

Is not religion all deeds and all reflection,

And that which is neither deed nor reflection, but a wonder and a surprise ever springing in the soul, even while the hands hew the stone or tend the loom?

Who can separate his faith from his actions, or his belief from his occupations?

Who can spread his hours before him, saying, "This for God and this for myself; This for my soul, and this other for my body?"

All your hours are wings that beat through space from self to self.

He who wears his morality but as his best garment were better naked.

The wind and the sun will tear no holes in his skin.

And he who defines his conduct by ethics imprisons his songbird in a cage.

The freest song comes not through bars and wires.

And he to whom worshipping is a window, to open but also to shut, has not yet visited the house of his soul whose windows are from dawn to dawn.

Your daily life is your temple and your religion.

Whenever you enter into it take with you your all.

Take the plough and the forge and the mallet and the lute,

The things you have fashioned in necessity or for delight.

For in reverie you cannot rise above your achievements nor fall lower than your failures.

And take with you all men:

For in adoration you cannot fly higher than their hopes nor humble yourself lower than their despair.

And if you would know God be not therefore a solver of riddles.

Rather look about you and you shall see Him playing with your children.

And look into space; you shall see Him walking in the cloud, outstretching His arms in the lightning and descending in rain.

You shall see Him smiling in flowers, then rising and waving His hands in trees.

From *The Prophet,* 1923

GIBRAN NEVER TOOK to churches or ritualized worship, though his maternal grandfather was a Maronite priest and his mother a devout Christian. "Religion? What is it? I know only life. Life means the field, the vineyard and the loom... The Church is within you. You yourself are your priest," he stated. By the 1920s, Gibran had developed his early impulses and flash revelations into an evolutionary cosmology. His religion was personal and deeply human; he saw God as the greater self seeking ever more exalted heights, even as man and earth are in pursuit of him. In the law of all matter as Gibran saw it, the higher emerges out of the lower, and all are lifted upward by God's desire for more of himself. Transcendental realities are already in this world, Gibran believed. They are within and available to man. "There are no keys," he explained to Mary Haskell, "because there are no doors. Here it is...Life...not locked away from us, but all around us." In the 1920s, Gibran became increasingly confident, encouraged by his growing fame in New York and his confirmed status in the Arab world and among the Arab expatriate community, which began to look to him as its figurehead.

On Good and Evil

THE ULTIMATE GOODNESS of man and the perfectibility of human nature were fundamental beliefs for Gibran. With his move to New York in 1912, Gibran's early influences from American transcendentalism—from the writing of Ralph Waldo Emerson, Walt Whitman and Henry David Thoreau, and the poetry of Maurice Maeterlinck and Algernon Charles Swinburne and others—began to develop into the evolutionary cosmology that defined his later vision. His view of mankind and the world was fundamentally optimistic. Evil is not the opposite of good, Gibran maintained. It is just a temporary state—a sign of the "not-yet" in man—that will be transformed by the force of "longing" for the "giant self" or the god-like being, which is within all of us. In "Satan," which was included in *The Tempests* (1920), Gibran dramatizes the nature of evil in an encounter between a priest and Satan. Here, he condemns the concepts of evil and the fallen state as fabrications perpetrated by the followers of Zoroaster in Ancient Persia, who believed in the good god of light (Mazda) and the evil god of darkness (Ahirman), a belief which seems to have infiltrated the Hebraic tradition and reappear later in religious institutions founded on fear.

AND ONE OF the elders of the city said, Speak to us of Good and Evil.

And he answered:

Of the good in you I can speak, but not of the evil.

For what is evil but good tortured by its own hunger and thirst?

Verily when good is hungry it seeks food even in dark caves, and when it thirsts, it drinks even of dead waters.

You are good when you are one with yourself.

Yet when you are not one with yourself you are not evil.

For a divided house is not a den of thieves; it is only a divided house.

And a ship without rudder may wander aimlessly among perilous isles yet sink not to the bottom.

You are good when you strive to give of yourself.

Yet you are not evil when you seek gain for yourself.

For when you strive for gain you are but a root that clings to the earth and sucks at her breast.

Surely the fruit cannot say to the root, "Be like me, ripe and full and ever giving of your abundance."

For to the fruit giving is a need, as receiving is a need to the root.

You are good when you are fully awake in your speech,

Yet you are not evil when you sleep while your tongue staggers without purpose.

And even stumbling speech may strengthen a weak tongue.

You are good when you walk to your goal firmly and with bold steps.

Yet you are not evil when you go thither limping.

Even those who limp go not backward.

But you who are strong and swift, see that you do not limp before the lame, deeming it kindness.

You are good in countless ways, and you are not evil when you are not good,

You are only loitering and sluggard.

Pity that the stags cannot teach swiftness to the turtles.

In your longing for your giant self lies your goodness: and that longing is in all of you.

But in some of you that longing is a torrent rushing with might to the sea, carrying the secrets of the hillsides and the songs of the forest.

And in others it is a flat stream that loses itself in angles and bends and lingers before it reaches the shore.

But let not him who longs much say to him who longs little, "Wherefore are you slow and halting?"

For the truly good ask not the naked, "Where is your garment?" nor the houseless, "What has befallen your house?"

From *The Prophet,* 1923

On God, Faith, and Religion

The first thought of God was an angel.
The first word of God was a man.

I too am visited by angels and devils, but I get rid of them.
When it is an angel I pray an old prayer, and he is bored;
When it is a devil I commit an old sin, and he passes me by.

He who can put his finger upon that which divides good from
evil is he who can touch the very hem of the garment of God.

Long ago there lived a Man who was crucified for being
too loving and too lovable.
And strange to relate I met him thrice yesterday.
The first time He was asking a policeman not to take a prostitute
to prison; the second time He was drinking wine with an outcast;
and the third time He was having a fistfight with a promoter
inside a church.

Faith is an oasis in the heart which will never be reached
by the caravan of thinking.

Once every hundred years Jesus of Nazareth meets Jesus of
the Christian in a garden among the hills of Lebanon.
And they talk long; and each time Jesus of Nazareth goes away
saying to Jesus of the Christian, "My friend, I fear we shall
never, never, agree."

There are three miracles of our Brother Jesus not yet recorded in
the Book: the first that He was a man like you and me; the
second that He had a sense of humor; and the third that He
knew He was a conqueror though conquered.

Crucified One, you are crucified upon my heart; and the nails
that pierce your hands pierce the walls of my heart.
And tomorrow when a stranger passes by this Golgotha
he will not know that two bled here.
He will deem it the blood of one man.

From *Sand and Foam*, 1926

## CHAPTER 5

LIFE, DEATH
and
REINCARNATION

Detail from *Departure and Return*, 1920, Wash drawing, 8½ x 11 inches (28 x 21.7 cm),
Gibran Museum, Bisharri, Lebanon

 On Death

Then Almitra spoke, saying, We would ask now of Death.

And he said:

You would know the secret of death.

But how shall you find it unless you seek it in the heart of life?

The owl whose night-bound eyes are blind unto the day cannot unveil the mystery of light.

If you would indeed behold the spirit of death, open your heart wide unto the body of life.

For life and death are one, even as the river and the sea are one.

In the depth of your hopes and desires lies your silent knowledge of the beyond;

And like seeds dreaming beneath the snow your heart dreams of spring.

Trust the dreams, for in them is hidden the gate to eternity.

Your fear of death is but the trembling of the shepherd when he stands before the king whose hand is to be laid upon him in honor.

Is the shepherd not joyful beneath his trembling, that he shall wear the mark of the king?

Yet is he not more mindful of his trembling?

For what is to die but to stand naked in the wind and to melt into the sun?

And what is to cease breathing, but to free the breath from its restless tides, that it may rise and expand and seek God unencumbered?

Only when you drink form the river of silence shall you indeed sing.

And when you have reached the mountain top, then you shall begin to climb.

And when the earth shall claim your limbs, then shall you truly dance.

From *The Prophet,* 1923

ON 4 APRIL 1902, Kahlil Gibran lost his younger sister Sultana, not long before his return from Beirut, where he was pursuing his Arabic studies. In the following year, he personally witnessed the death of his half-brother Peter (on 12 March) and then his mother Kamila (on 28 June). "My poor Prophet (whom I am anxiously watching)...is going through a soul-forcing process rare to witness," wrote Josephine Peabody of the young man barely on the cusp of his ambitions to her confidante Mary Mason. Gibran's innate faith in the immortality of the soul and the unbreakable bonds of love—which not even death could sever—helped early on to form his views on death, the immortality of the soul and reincarnation. "Dust of the Ages and the Eternal Fire" (included in *Nymphs of the Valley,* 1906) describes two lovers united by the goddess of love Astarte in 116 BCE who are reunited in a new incarnation in 1890. Upon hearing of the death of his father while in Paris, Gibran wrote to Mary Haskell, on 23 June 1909, "I know, dear Mary, that they live. They live a life more real, more beautiful than ours. They are nearer to God than we are."

Detail from *Death of the Mother*, 1916, Wash drawing, 11 x 8½ inches (21.5 x 28 cm),
Gibran Museum, Bisharri, Lebanon

On Pain

THROUGH HIS PERSONAL example, Gibran showed us how pain is not only to be endured as an inescapable part of life, but can be transmuted into creative energy. He knew pain very early in life. Perhaps it began with the physical discomfort of dislocating his shoulder as a child of ten or eleven—"and I stayed strapped to that cross for forty days," he wrote, using an image which he would associate with Christ. Then there was the heartache of uprooting from Bisharri, a village that transformed in his memory into an image of beauty and serenity, sacred cedars and the holy spirit. A stranger in a strange land, Gibran then lost his sister, half-brother and mother in two years. This left him bereft, stranded with his remaining sister and his burning ambition. Around that time most of Gibran's drawings and paintings were destroyed in Fred Holland Day's studio where they were being exhibited. From then on Gibran, inhabiting the in-between world of East and West, man and myth, present and future, created his own universe, populating it with powerful consolatory symbols, words and images. Mary Haskell commented on how inspiring his imperturbability and resilience were in the face of setback or hardship. Yet perhaps the flames were burning quietly; Gibran guarded his privacy jealously.

AND A WOMAN spoke, saying, Tell us of Pain. And he said:

Your pain is the breaking of the shell that encloses your understanding.

Even as the stone of the fruit must break, that its heart may stand in the sun, so must you know pain.

And could you keep your heart in wonder at the daily miracles of your life, your pain would not seem less wondrous than your joy;

And you would accept the seasons of your heart, even as you have always accepted the seasons that pass over your fields.

And you would watch with serenity through the winters of your grief.

Much of your pain is self-chosen.

It is the bitter potion by which the physician within you heals your sick self.

Therefore trust the physician, and drink his remedy in silence and tranquillity:

For his hand, though heavy and hard, is guided by the tender hand of the Unseen,

And the cup he brings, though it burn your lips, has been fashioned of the clay which the Potter has moistened with His own sacred tears.

From *The Prophet,* 1923

A Tear and a Smile

I would not exchange the sorrows of my heart for the jubilees of the masses, nor would I grant that the tears that flow from my parts, engulfed in gloom, be turned into burgeoning laughter. I would but for my life to remain a tear and a smile: a tear that would purify my heart and make me to understand life's hidden meanings and ambiguities, and a smile that brings me nearer to my kin and becomes my symbol for the worship of the gods; a tear with which to join the crushed of heart in solidarity, and a smile that becomes a visible token of my joy in existence.

Sooner would I perish of longing than live in dullness! Would that the depths of my soul be consumed by an eternal, unappeasable appetite for love and beauty. For I have looked all around and seen that those who are satisfied are the most wretched of all people, and are enslaved by their own earthiness. I have heard the burning sighs of unrequited love and I have found them sweeter than love satisfied.

As evening approaches, the rose folds its petals and sleeps in the embrace of her yearnings. But with the approach of the morn, she parts her lips to receive the kiss of the sun. For the life of a flower is a longing and a fulfilment, a tear and a smile.

The sea's waters become vapor and rise, gathering into a cloud. The cloud floats above the hills and the valleys until it meets a gentle breeze and then it falls, weeping toward the fields. Only then does it join the running streams and return to the sea, its home and origin. The life of a cloud is a separation and a union, a tear and a smile.

And so is it for the spirit. The individual spirit becomes separated from the greater spirit and sojourns in the world of matter, a wandering cloud over the mountains of sorrow and the plains of joy, until it meets the subtle breeze of death. The spirit thus sojourns until it returns to its origin; to the Greater Sea of Love and Beauty; to God!

From *A Tear and a Smile,* 1914 (trans. Ayman A. El-Desouky)

IN THE SAME BREATH, Gibran would write profusely on joy and sorrow, and on how beauty is found in the balance between these two aspects of existence. Beyond the Romantic imagery, joy and sorrow were not simply emotions to Gibran, but conditions of being human. "Beauty is that harmony between joy and sorrow which begins in our holy of holies and ends beyond the scope of our imagination. To the body it is a trial; to the spirit, a gift," Mikhail Naimy reported him as saying. The harmony of which Gibran speaks is the longing that bonds the spirit of an individual to the greater spirit. Though such equanimity is reminiscent of Buddhist doctrine, Gibran's view is more informed by the mystical traditions of Islam, especially by the work of the Islamic jurist, theologian and mystic philosopher al-Ghazali (1058–1111) and the Arab mystic poet Ibn al-Farid (1181–1235) on whom he wrote essays. In these traditions, seemingly contradictory states are dissolved in the burning longing for the beloved or God. Here, joy and sorrow are to be endured alike for they are equal signs of separation from the beloved. "And so does the spirit become separated from the greater spirit to move in the world of matter," Gibran explains toward the end of this extract.

 # Revelation

U PON A NIGHT, and as the hour advanced and slumber cast wide its cloak upon the face of the earth, I rose from my bedding and walked toward the sea, whispering to myself: "Surely, the sea never sleeps, and in its wakeful company there must be some consolation for a sleepless spirit."

I reached the shore as the mist had descended from its mountain heights and covered those regions, as a grey veil covers the face of a beautiful maiden. I stood there, gazing into the night toward those never ending armies of waves, listening to their jubilations and reflecting on the primordial force that lies behind them; that same force that races over the tempests and erupts in volcanoes, even as it smiles on the lips of roses and synchronizes with the music of running brooks.

After a while, I turned around and, upon a sudden, I beheld three ghost-like figures seated on a rock nearby, enveloped in a swathe of mist that enfolded them but did not render them invisible. I walked in their direction, slowly, something in them forcing me to draw nearer, even against my will.

And when I became but a few paces away from them, I stood there, transfixed in the spot, as by some magical power that froze my will while unleashing all the powers of my imagination.

Exactly at that moment, one of the figures rose and, in a voice I imagined could only have issued from the depths of the sea, said:

"Life without Love is a tree without blossom and barren of fruit. And Love without Beauty is a flower without scent and a seedless fruit. Life, Love and Beauty—three entities in One Self—independent, boundless, indomitable, indivisible."

He spoke thus and sat in his place.

The second figure then sprang to his feet and bellowed in a voice like the roar of deep oceans:

"Life without Rebellion is like the passing of seasons with no spring. And Rebellion without Right is the spring of barren, desolate wastes. Life, Rebellion and Right—three entities in One Self—indivisible, indomitable."

Upon that, the third figure also sprang to his feet, and in the voice of thunder, said:

"Life without Freedom is a body without spirit. And Freedom without Reason is a spirit bewildered. Life, Freedom and Reason—three entities in One Self—primordial, everlasting, undiminished."

Upon the which, all three rose and, together, in fearsome, awe-inspiring voices said:

"Love and what it engenders, Rebellion and what it brings to existence, Freedom and what it nurtures—three aspects of God—and God is the reasoning conscience of the world."

Thereupon fell a complete and utter silence, brimming with the soft fluttering of invisible wings and quickened with the movements of ethereal beings. I shut my eyes, taking in the echoes of what I had just heard. When I opened them and looked once more, I found but the sea shrouded in mist. I drew nearer to the rock where the three figures had been sitting, but all I could see was a pillar of perfumed smoke rising up toward the firmaments.

From *The Tempests*, 1920 (trans. Ayman A. El-Desouky)

Third God

PUBLISHED THREE weeks before his death in 1931, *The Earth Gods* presents Gibran's epic vision of the cycle of life, with its forces of denial, affirmation and reconciliation. This underwent a long gestation, dating back as far as 1914. Three gods take turns to present Gibran's views, and the drama ends with a reconciliation brought about through the power of love. Mikhail Naimy, who witnessed Gibran's last moments, records how Gibran brought the manuscript to him asking him to read it aloud, which Naimy did after a long discussion over beauty. Gibran passionately argued, "Perhaps we are nearer to Him each time we try to divide Him and find Him indivisible. Yet do I say that art, through drawing a line between the beautiful and the ugly, is the nearest way to God." In Gibran's art, God is characteristically visualized as the God-Mother, the creative spirit as All-Mother of the Universe. He rejected the masculinization of God in most religions. "To me He is as much a mother as He is a Father," Gibran told Naimy on another occasion. "He is both the father and the mother in one; and Woman is the God-Mother. The God-Father may be reached through the mind or the imagination. But the God-Mother can be reached through the heart only—through love." The trinity of figures is a running motif in Gibran's work.

OH, THE AFFLICTION of knowing,
The starless veil of prying and questioning
Which we have laid upon the world;
And the challenge to human forbearance!
We would lay under a stone a waxen shape
And say, It is a thing of clay,
And in clay let it find its end.
We would hold in our hands a white flame
And say in our heart,
It is a fragment of ourselves returning,
A breath of our breath that had escaped,
And now haunts our hands and lips for more fragrance.
Earth gods, my brothers,
High upon the mountain,
We are still earthbound,
Through man desiring the golden hours of man's destiny.
Shall our wisdom ravish beauty from his eyes?
Shall our measures subdue his passion to stillness,
Or to our own passion?

From *The Earth Gods*, 1931

The Heavenly Mother (from *The Forerunner*), 1920, Pencil on woven paper, 14½ x 22¼ inches (56.5 x 36.8 cm), The Telfair Museum of Art, Savannah, Georgia

 # The River

A POTENT SYMBOL for Gibran, the river represents life, both for individuals and collectively. It also conveys Gibran's fundamental insight that just as the river and sea become one, so life and death are indivisible, too. Death is the great liberator, he maintained, when we rush into the river that is God or the greater spirit. Gibran believed that after death we retain consciousness and our individual evolution continues. "The soul never loses its inherent properties when it reaches God," Gibran wrote to Mary Haskell on 10 February 1916. "Salt does not lose its saltness in the sea," he continued to explain, "its properties are inherent and eternal. The soul will retain consciousness, the hunger for more of itself and the desire for that which is beyond itself. The soul will retain those properties through all eternity, and like other elements in nature it will remain absolute. The absolute seeks more absoluteness, more crystallization." These statements are some of the clearest expressions of the tenets of Gibran's vision: that the personality survives after death, that the soul is a higher form of matter, that nature or the spirit of the earth shares the same desire as man for higher forms of being, and that God, too, evolves.

I N THE VALLEY of Kadisha where the mighty river flows, two little streams met and spoke to one another.

One stream said, "How came you, my friend, and how was your path?"

And the other answered, "My path was most encumbered. The wheel of the mill was broken, and the master farmer who used to conduct me from my channel to his plants, is dead. I struggled down oozing with the filth of those who do naught but sit and bake their laziness in the sun. But how was your path, my brother?"

And the other stream answered and said, "Mine was a different path. I came down the hills among fragrant flowers and shy willows; men and women drank of me with silvery cups, and little children paddled their rosy feet at my edges, and there was laughter all about me, and there were sweet songs. What a pity that your path was not so happy."

At that moment the river spoke with a loud voice and said, "Come in, come in, we are going to the sea. Come in, come in, speak no more. Be with me now. We are going to the sea. Come in, come in, for in me you shall forget you wanderings, sad or gay. Come in, come in. And you and I will forget all our ways when we reach the heart of our mother the sea."

From *The Wanderer: His Parables and Sayings,* 1932

Detail from *Crucified*, 1918, (published in *Twenty Drawings*, 1919), Wash drawing,
8¾ x 10 inches (25 x 20 cm), Gibran Museum, Bisharri, Lebanon

Virgin and Child with St. Anne, c.1510, Leonardo da Vinci, Oil on wood,
51 x 66 inches (16.8 x 13.0 cm), Louvre, Paris, France. Gibran ranked da Vinci as one
of the founders of new paths for humanity, because he "wanted to paint what men
could not understand" and he "painted with mind." He thought this painting of
St. Anna, Mary, Jesus and the Lamb to be "the most wonderful picture in the world."

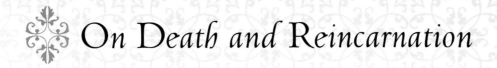

On Death and Reincarnation

Death is not nearer to the aged than to the newborn;
neither is life.

Mayhap a funeral among men is a wedding feast
among the angels.

A forgotten reality may die and leave in its will seven thousand
actualities and facts to be spent in its funeral and
the building of a tomb.

I said to Life, "I would hear Death speak."
And Life raised her voice a little higher and said,
"You hear him now."

When you have solved all the mysteries of life you long for
death, for it is but another mystery of life.

All those who have lived in the past live with us now.
Surely none of us would be an ungracious host.

From *Sand and Foam,* 1926

## CHAPTER 6

SPIRIT, TRUTH
and
WISDOM

Detail from *Joy and Sorrow*, 1920–1923, Watercolor,
8½ x 11 inches (28 x 21.5 cm), Gibran Museum, Bisharri, Lebanon

❧ You are Spirits

THOUGH GIBRAN'S style reflects biblical rhythms and cadences, both his English and Arabic writing was richly informed by the Qur'an and Islamic mystical traditions. These influences appear most often as striking images—"the winged self" or "the breath of His breath"—which Gibran employed to create a knowing, confident tone of voice. In this extract, the image of flames held in lamps is a direct reference to the verses of light in the Qur'an: "GOD is the light of the heavens and the earth. His light is like unto that of a concave mirror before which there is a lamp, and the lamp is placed inside a glass container... Light upon light. GOD guides to His light whomsoever He wills." (24:35). The inspiration of the Qur'an is also evident in the night of power mentioned here— the night of revelation in which the Spirit and angels descend to earth. Gibran felt that the image of light reflecting light was a moving metaphor for our relation to the divine. But he believed also that while mankind is essentially spiritual, we are of the body too, and through the body we connect with the spirit of the earth.

THEN HE WENT forth with the woman, he and the nine, even unto the marketplace, and he spoke to the people, his friends and his neighbors, and there was joy in their hearts and upon their eyelids.

And he said: "You grow in sleep, and live your fuller life in your dreaming. For all your days are spent in thanksgiving for that which you have received in the stillness of the night.

"Oftentimes you think and speak of night as the season of rest, yet in truth night is the season of seeking and finding.

"The day gives unto you the power of knowledge and teaches your fingers to become versed in the art of receiving; but it is night that leads you to the treasure-house of Life.

"The sun teaches to all things that grow their longing for the light. But it is night that raises them to the stars.

"It is indeed the stillness of the night that weaves a wedding veil over the trees in the forest, and the flowers in the garden, and then spreads the lavish feast and makes ready the nuptial chamber; and in that holy silence tomorrow is conceived in the womb of Time.

"Thus it is with you, and thus, in seeking, you find meat and fulfilment. And though at dawn your awakening erases the memory, the board of dreams is for ever spread, and the nuptial chamber waiting."

And he was silent for a space, and they also, awaiting his word. Then he spoke again, saying: "You are spirits though you move in bodies; and, like oil that burns in the dark, you are flames though held in lamps.

"If you were naught save bodies, then my standing before you and speaking unto you would be but emptiness, even as the dead calling unto the dead. But this is not so. All that is deathless in you is free unto the day and the night and cannot be housed nor fettered, for this is the will of the Most High. You are His breath even as the wind that shall be neither caught nor caged. And I also am the breath of His breath."

And he went from their midst walking swiftly and entered again into the Garden.

And Sarkis, he who was the half-doubter, spoke and said: "And what of ugliness, Master? You speak never of ugliness."

And Almustafa answered him, and there was a whip in his words, and he said: "My friend, what man shall call you inhospitable if he shall pass by your house, yet would not knock at your door?

"And who shall deem you deaf and unmindful if he shall speak to you in a strange tongue of which you understand nothing?

"Is it not that which you have never striven to reach, into whose heart you have never desired to enter, that you deem ugliness?

"If ugliness is aught, indeed, it is but the scales upon our eyes, and the wax filling our ears.

"Call nothing ugly, my friend, save the fear of a soul in the presence of its own memories."

From *The Garden of the Prophet*, 1933

An Apparition of Wisdom

THE YOUNG GIBRAN'S relationship with Josephine Peabody was fueled by intense poetic-transcendentalist thoughts. He rushed to her with drawings and poems, and they spent evenings reading aloud, pondering symbols and allegories, and discussing poetry and mythology. Gibran was enduring distressing times, buffeted by family deaths and poverty, and so too was Josephine with her family's financial struggles and constant house-moving. They sought refuge in each other's company and in a fiercely imaginative world. In "The Queen of Fantasy" and "Before the Throne of Beauty," as in this piece, (all from the 1914 collection *A Tear and a Smile*), muses appear, modeled after Josephine, to counsel and console the young poet. On 21 November 1902 she reflected on her role: "I am a prism that catches the light a moment. It is the light that gladdens, not the prism. And yet for that moment, the prism...the accidental woman, becomes perforce...a messenger of God." The advice given here by Wisdom to take to the woods is heeded later by the youth in *The Processions* (1919), who speaks as though he and nature were one. Gibran believed that wisdom is imaginative knowledge, spiritually imparted either in the mind or through communion with nature. This wisdom equips one to rise beyond oneself and inspire others.

IN THE STILLNESS of night, Wisdom appeared to me and stood by my bed. Even as a loving mother, She gazed at me and, wiping my tears tenderly, She said: "I heard the cry of your soul and have come to console it! Open your heart and spread it before me that I may fill it with light! Ask me and I shall show you the way of truth!"

And I said: "O Wisdom, who am I? And how is it I arrived in such a fearful place? Such mighty hopes and the many books and strange designs, what are these, O Wisdom? And what are these thoughts that pass over me like a flock of pigeons? And this mode of speech, what is it, strung into verse by the rhythm of longing and then broken up into the prose of pleasure? And what manner are such outcomes, at once making me feel sad and filling me with joy; embracing my spirit and beguiling my heart? Whence these eyes that stare right through me, exposing my depths and yet ignoring my woes? What are these bewailing voices that lament my days and turn my own smallness into rhythmic incantation? What youthfulness is this that messes about with my longings and recklessly plays with my emotions; this youth that forgets the deeds of yesterday, tarries with today's lack of consequence and hurries not the morrow?"

"What world is this that leads me to where I know not and only admits but what demeans me? What is this earth that opens wide to swallow bodies and takes to its bosom the ambitious? Who is this man who remains passionate for happiness even as he perishes in the abyss; this man who seeks the kiss of life even as he is threshed by death? This man who trades a year of remorse for a moment of pleasure; who gives in to slumber even as dreams call him; who ties himself to the waterwheels of ignorance only to flow with its water into the bay of darkness? I pray, what are all these and more, O Wisdom?"

Then She answered saying: "You the mortal, you want to see the world with the eyes of a god and fathom the secrets of a world to come with the probings of a mortal thought. Such folly! Go you out, go into the wilderness and observe how the bee hovers above the flower and the eagle swoops down on his prey. Enter you into your neighbor's hearth and see you the child blinking at the firelight and the mother busied at her house chores. Be you like the bee and do not waste the days of your spring eyeing the works of the eagle. Be like the child and rejoice in the warmth of the firelight, and let your mother go about her own business. All that you see has been and will always be for your own sake."

"The many books and strange designs and beautiful thoughts are but the apparitions of those who have gone ahead of you. The speech whose words you wrought is what forges the bond between you and your fellow mortals. The at once saddening and joy-filling consequences and effects are but the seeds sown by the past in the burrows of the soul for the benefit of the future. That youthfulness, which wreaks havoc on your desires, is what pries open your heart for the light. This earth, with its mouth forever wide open, is what delivers you from the enslavement of your body. This world, which leads your path is your own heart, for all that you deem a world unto itself is but of your own heart. This man, whom you deem benighted and insignificant, is the one sent by God to learn joy through sorrow and knowledge out of darkness..."

Wisdom then placed her hand on my feverish forehead and said: "Go forth and never tarry, for forward is the secret of perfection. Walk forth and do not fear the thorns on your path, for they do not spill but fouled blood!"

From *A Tear and a Smile*, 1914 (trans. Ayman A. El-Desouky)

Solitude, 1912, Oil on canvas, 28 x 20 inches (50.5 x 71 cm),
Gibran Museum, Bisharri, Lebanon

On Time

ASTRONOMY HELD a deep fascination for Gibran, and he was elated when Mary Haskell presented him with a meteorite rock from the Diablo Canyon in Arizona, which he kept under his pillow until his death. It was the "most wonderful thing" anyone had ever given to him, he would say. Gibran felt that the rock brought him in contact with timeless, measureless space, a place "crowded with Infinities, and as *grim* and as heavy as Birth and Loneliness." The gift inspired many discussions and a piece of writing entitled "The Astronomer," which he included in *The Madman* (1918). Gibran longed for the ability to live fully in each fresh moment, while keeping an eye open to the future and its possibilities. For only then, he believed, could he rework his past, recreating aspects of himself that he wished to change (these he referred to as his "former selves.") This desire to live in the present moment, though abundantly expressed in the mystical writings and Romantic poems Gibran loved to read, is, in fact, what constitutes the modernist impulse in him. For Gibran, modern individuals must seek to ground themselves not in the past or some metaphysical system but in the present and their own personal potential.

AND AN ASTRONOMER said, Master, what of Time? And he answered:

You would measure time the measureless and the immeasurable.

You would adjust your conduct and even direct the course of your spirit according to hours and seasons.

Of time you would make a stream upon whose bank you would sit and watch its flowing.

Yet the timeless in you is aware of life's timelessness,

And knows that yesterday is but today's memory and tomorrow is today's dream.

And that that which sings and contemplates in you is still dwelling within the bounds of that first moment which scattered the stars into space.

Who among you does not feel that his power to love is boundless?

And yet who does not feel that very love, though boundless, encompassed within the centre of his being, and moving not from love thought to love thought, nor from love deeds to other love deeds?

And is not time even as love is, undivided and spaceless?

But if in you thought you must measure time into seasons, let each season encircle all the other seasons,

And let today embrace the past with remembrance and the future with longing.

From *The Prophet*, 1923

When My Sorrow was Born

THOUGH HE FACED poverty and personal tragedy during his early years in Boston, Gibran eventually secured financial security and found fame in New York as his status as poet, artist and thinker grew both within America and in the Arab world. However, as he grew older, Gibran became increasingly hermetic in his inclinations. Indeed, throughout his life, he was only ever happy when he felt in the presence of his "larger self"—when an event, encounter or creative act contributed to his potential for personal growth. Often, these moments of presence when he felt the depths rising out of him, came during experiences of pain and sorrow. He believed that such episodes cleared away life's little cares and brought with them fresh insight and perspective. Gibran's creative genius was his ability to articulate the ways in which various shades of sorrow and loneliness, loss and disillusion can refine one's sensibilities and regenerate the spirit. Gibran's writings before *The Prophet* in 1923, which began to sound a more positive note, offer many illustrations of such downbeat moods. Drawings from that period are allegorical presentations of similar existential states. Still Gibran wished to impart "the large quiet— that peace of Earth," as he told Mary on 23 December 1914.

Self-Absorbed, pre-1914, Oil on canvas, 24¾ x 34 inches (86.5 x 63 cm), Gibran Museum, Bisharri, Lebanon

WHEN MY SORROW was born I nursed it with care, and watched over it with loving tenderness.

And my Sorrow grew like all living things, strong and beautiful and full of wondrous delights.

And we loved one another, my Sorrow and I, and we loved the world about us; for Sorrow had a kindly heart and mine was kindly with Sorrow.

And when we conversed, my Sorrow and I, our days were winged and our nights were girdled with dreams; for Sorrow had an eloquent tongue, and mine was eloquent with Sorrow.

And when we sang together, my Sorrow and I, our neighbors sat at their windows and listened; for our songs were deep as the sea and our melodies were full of strange memories.

And when we walked together, my Sorrow and I, people gazed at us with gentle eyes and whispered in words of exceeding sweetness. And there were those who looked with envy upon us, for Sorrow was a noble thing and I was proud with Sorrow.

But my Sorrow died, like all living things, and alone I am left to muse and ponder.

And now when I speak my words fall heavily upon my ears.

And when I sing my songs my neighbors come not to listen.

And when I walk the streets no one looks at me.

Only in my sleep I hear voices saying in pity, "See, there lies the man whose Sorrow is dead."

From *The Madman: His Parables and Poems*, 1918

Toward the Infinite, pre-1914, Oil on canvas, 24 x 18 inches (45.5 x 61 cm),
Gibran Museum, Bisharri, Lebanon

And When My Joy was Born

JOY AND SORROW in Gibran's view of the world, go hand in hand, just like life and death, space and time, body and soul, matter and form, and man and God. In each case one emerges from the other. In a state of sorrow, for example, one is better able to face oneself calmly, away from other people, and so to achieve a better understanding both of oneself and others, a prerequisite of joyfulness. Gibran felt able to give himself more fully to his creative work when experiencing intense emotional states, such as sorrow, pain and longing. He felt they helped him to endure the loneliness essential for creation. Gibran perhaps knew only two kinds of joy: the delight of creation and the bliss of recognition by others during deep moments of personal connection. Joy for Gibran was not a private state; it demanded to be shared, and hence it belonged more to his social self than his private world. "Kahlil was looking lovely in every one of his thousand aspects," Mary Haskell confided to her journal on 30 August 1920, "he was full of that radiant smile of his, the freshest, gentlest, brightest play of light in any human face. He has written the 'Farewell of the Prophet,' and read it to me."

AND WHEN MY Joy was born I held it in my arms and stood on the housetop shouting, "Come ye, my neighbors, come and see, for Joy this day is born unto me. Come and behold this gladsome thing that laugheth in the sun."

But none of my neighbors came to look upon my Joy, and great was my astonishment.

And every day for seven moons I proclaimed my Joy from the house-top—and yet no one heeded me. And my Joy and I were alone, unsought and unvisited.

Then my Joy grew pale and weary because no other heart but mine held its loveliness and no other lips kissed its lips.

Then my Joy died of isolation.

And now I only remember my dead Joy in remembering my dead Sorrow. But memory is an autumn leaf that murmurs a while in the wind and then is heard no more.

From *The Madman: His Parables and Poems,* 1918

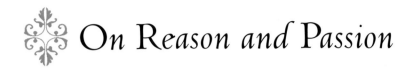

On Reason and Passion

AND THE PRIESTESS spoke again and said: Speak to us of Reason and Passion.

And he answered saying:

Your soul is oftentimes a battlefield, upon which your reason and your judgment wage war against your passion and your appetite.

Would that I could be the peacemaker in your soul, that I might turn the discord and the rivalry of your elements into oneness and melody.

But how shall I, unless you yourselves be also the peacemakers, nay, the lovers of all your elements?

Your reason and your passion are the rudder and the sails of your seafaring soul.

If either your sails or your rudder be broken, you can but toss and drift, or else be held at a standstill in mid-seas.

For reason, ruling alone, is a force confining; and passion, unattended, is a flame that burns to its own destruction.

Therefore let your soul exalt your reason to the height of passion; that it may sing;

And let it direct your passion with reason, that your passion may live through its own daily resurrection, and like the phœnix rise above its own ashes.

I would have you consider your judgment and your appetite even as you would two loved guests in your house.

Surely you would not honor one guest above the other; for he who is more mindful of one loses the love and the faith of both.

Among the hills, when you sit in the cool shade of the white poplars, sharing the peace and serenity of distant fields and meadows—then let your heart say in silence, "God rests in reason."

And when the storm comes, and the mighty wind shakes the forest, and thunder and lightning proclaim the majesty of the sky,—then let your heart say in awe, "God moves in passion."

And since you are a breath in God's sphere, and a leaf in God's forest, you too should rest in reason and move in passion.

From *The Prophet,* 1923

IN ARABIC TRADITION, the heart is "the house of the Lord," and knowledge experienced through the heart—the receptacle of revelation—is considered higher than pure reason. This is the way of the *Sufi* or mystic, who in a state of heightened meditation and trance, achieved through the repetition of words or movements in *zikr* circles, retains the clarity to contemplate divine signs. Gibran favored this tradition of *Sufism*, as practiced by al-Ghazali (1058–1111), to the habits of *Sufis* given to total self-effacement, such as the famous 10th-century al-Hallaj, who was eventually executed for such proclamations as "No one in my cloak but God." The logic in Gibran's writings takes the form of passionate knowing; a strong emotion guides his thoughts, often conveyed using striking imagery, into free-form speculation that allows him to explore ideas beyond received tradition. The poet in Gibran never settled for being a mouthpiece for ideas; he preferred to articulate them using the power of emotions. When Gibran engaged with abstract values, as in many pieces in *A Tear and a Smile* (1914), he always personified them, then engaged them in dialogue. In *Sand and Foam* (1926) Gibran wrote, "there lies a green field between the scholar and the poet; should the scholar cross it he becomes a wise man; should the poet cross it, he becomes a prophet."

On Pleasure

THE SPIRIT OF NEW YORK inspired and invigorated Gibran, with its diverse population, high energy levels and fast-paced lifestyle. Life in Boston was more social, revolving around artistic circles and high society events, where as a talented entertainer and conversationalist, Gibran was a popular guest. However, he never felt fulfilled in such situations. Judging by the many accounts in Mary Haskell's journals and his correspondence with intimate friends, Gibran's ultimate pleasure came from cultivating his "aloneness" during solitary walks and brief escapades out of New York and Boston to the nearby countryside and mountains. In these calming periods of solitude he would reminisce about his childhood experiences in the Cedar Mountains of Lebanon and spend many hours musing and drawing his observations. Gibran confessed to Mary on 5 April 1914, "as I grow older, Mary, the hermit in me becomes more determined. Life is a vision full of infinite, sweet possibilities and fulfilments." These "sweet possibilities" increasingly consumed Gibran in "The Hermitage," his studio in New York, as he attempted to turn the many shadows flitting in his heart and mind into words and images.

THEN A HERMIT, who visited the city once a year, came forth and said, Speak to us of Pleasure.

And he answered, saying:

Pleasure is a freedom song,

But it is not freedom.

It is the blossoming of your desires,

But it is not their fruit.

It is a depth calling unto a height,

But it is not the deep nor the high.

It is the caged taking wing,

But it is not space encompassed.

Ay, in very truth, pleasure is a freedom song.

And I fain would have you sing it with fullness of heart; yet I would not have you lose your hearts in the singing.

Some of your youth seek pleasure as if it were all, and they are judged and rebuked.

I would not judge nor rebuke them. I would have them seek.

For they shall find pleasure, but not her alone:

Seven are her sisters, and the least of them is more beautiful than pleasure.

Have you not heard of the man who was digging in the earth for roots and found a treasure?

And some of your elders remember pleasures with regret like wrongs committed in drunkenness.

But regret is the beclouding of the mind and not its chastisement.

They should remember their pleasures with gratitude, as they would the harvest of a summer.

Yet if it comforts them to regret, let them be comforted.

And there are among you those who are neither young to seek nor old to remember;
And in their fear of seeking and remembering they shun all pleasures, lest they neglect the spirit or offend against it.
But even in their forgoing is their pleasure.
And thus they too find a treasure though they dig for roots with quivering hands.
But tell me, who is he that can offend the spirit?
Shall the nightingale offend the stillness of the night, or the firefly the stars?
And shall your flame or your smoke burden the wind?
Think you the spirit is a still pool which you can trouble with a staff?

Oftentimes in denying yourself pleasure you do but store the desire in the recesses of your being.
Who knows but that which seems omitted today, waits for tomorrow?
Even your body knows its heritage and its rightful need and will not be deceived.
And your body is the harp of your soul,
And it is yours to bring forth sweet music from it or confused sounds.

And now you ask in your heart, "How shall we distinguish that which is good in pleasure from that which is not good?"
Go to your fields and your gardens, and you shall learn that it is the pleasure of the bee to gather honey of the flower,
But it is also the pleasure of the flower to yield its honey to the bee.
For to the bee a flower is a fountain of life,
And to the flower a bee is a messenger of love,
And to both, bee and flower, the giving and the receiving of pleasure is a need and an ecstasy.

People of Orphalese, be in your pleasures like the flowers and the bees.

From *The Prophet*, 1923

Betwixt Truth and Fantasy

LIFE TOSSES US hither and thither, and destiny moves us from one environs to the other, and we see not save what stands an obstacle on our path, and we hear not save the voice that frightens us.

Beauty reveals itself to us in the height of its glory, but all we do is draw near and defile the hems of its garb and wrest from upon its head the crown of its purity!

Love passes in front of us, clad in all its tenderness, but we deny it in fear and we hide in the recesses of darkness, or we follow it and commit all that is evil in its name! Even the wise among us bear it like a heavy yoke, and yet he is even more gentle than the fragrant breath of flowers and gentler even than the breezes of Lebanon!

Wisdom stands on street corners and calls to us above the heads of them that witness, but we deem her a thing without merit and we despise them that follow!

Freedom summons us to its sumptuous banquet that we may savor its excellent wine and culinary fares; we arrive thither and immediately fall upon it, gluttonously filling our bellies so that the noble banquet turns into a spectacle for ignominy and an occasion for self-abasement!

Nature extends to us her hand in friendship, bidding us to enjoy her beauty; but we fear its serenity and take refuge in the city, and there breed and multiply upon one another, trampling upon one another like a flock of sheep fleeing before a prowling wolf!

Truth visits us, drawn by the smile of a babe or the kiss of a beloved, and we slam the doors of our emotions shut before her and abandon her as only the unclean wayward would!

The human heart asks succor of us, and the spirit calls, yet we remain even more still than the unmoved stone, heeding not nor understanding. And should one of us hear the cry of his own heart and heed the call of his own spirit, we shun him as one possessed and wash our hands of his blood!

Thus pass the nights in heedlessness and the days turn upon us, and we remain fearful of the nights and apprehensive of the days. We remain predisposed to dust, and yet the gods claim us! We pass before the bread of life, and hunger feeds upon our strength. O how we love life, and how remote is life from us!

From *A Tear and a Smile,* 1914 (trans. Ayman A. El-Desouky)

DURING HIS TIME in Boston, before moving to New York in 1912, Gibran's Romantic leanings led him to the fundamental belief that change could trigger a state of hopefulness. He maintained that one must open oneself up to experiences and embrace them, releasing the tension that builds up in the mind, heart and body when we resist fate. Gibran himself let go of tension in the presence of nature and by contemplating love, truth and beauty. He warned that those who did not do so would face a life of dissatisfaction or inhabit a mirage. Gibran felt that he must fill his time only with those activities, thoughts and emotions that fed his higher calling: bettering his understanding of himself and expressing that awareness in his art and writing. "I am attending to one big thing in life," Gibran told Mary Haskell on Christmas Day 1912, "I can't stop for details alien to it." For Gibran, the line between truth and fantasy was drawn not by knowledge of facts or abstract principles but by relevance to personal growth. Truth was everything that enabled self-knowledge and the understanding of others; the rest was fantasy.

On Spirit, Truth, Wisdom

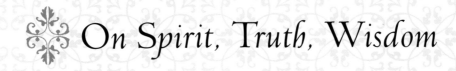

Do not the spirits who dwell in the ether envy man his pain?

Even the most winged spirit cannot escape physical necessity.

A hermit is one who renounces the world of fragments that he
may enjoy the world wholly and without interruption.

Half of what I say is meaningless; but I say it so that
the other half may reach you.

The reality of the other person is not in what he reveals to
you, but in what he cannot reveal to you.
Therefore, if you would understand him, listen not to what he
says but rather to what he does not say.

Should you really open your eyes and see, you would behold
your image in all images.
And should you open your ears and listen, you would hear
your own voice in all voices.

Silence, 1922, Watercolor, 22½ x 28¼ inches (72 x 57 cm),
Gibran Museum, Bisharri, Lebanon

The deep and the high go to the depth or to the height in a
straight line; only the spacious can move in circles.

Should you really open your eyes and see, you would behold
your image in all images.
And should you open your ears and listen, you would hear
your own voice in all voices.

It takes two of us to discover truth: one to utter it
and one to understand it.

Though the wave of words is forever upon us, yet our depth
is forever silent.

Many a doctrine is like a window pane.
We see truth through it but it divides us from truth.

How noble is the sad heart who would sing a joyous song
with joyous hearts.

Every dragon gives birth to a St. George who slays it.

No longing remains unfulfilled.

If you would possess you must not claim.

Only great sorrow or great joy can reveal your truth.
If you would be revealed you must either dance naked in the sun,
or carry your cross.

You see but your shadow when you turn your back to the sun.

We often borrow from our tomorrows to pay our debts
to our yesterdays.

Even the masks of life are masks of deeper mystery.

From *Sand and Foam*, 1926

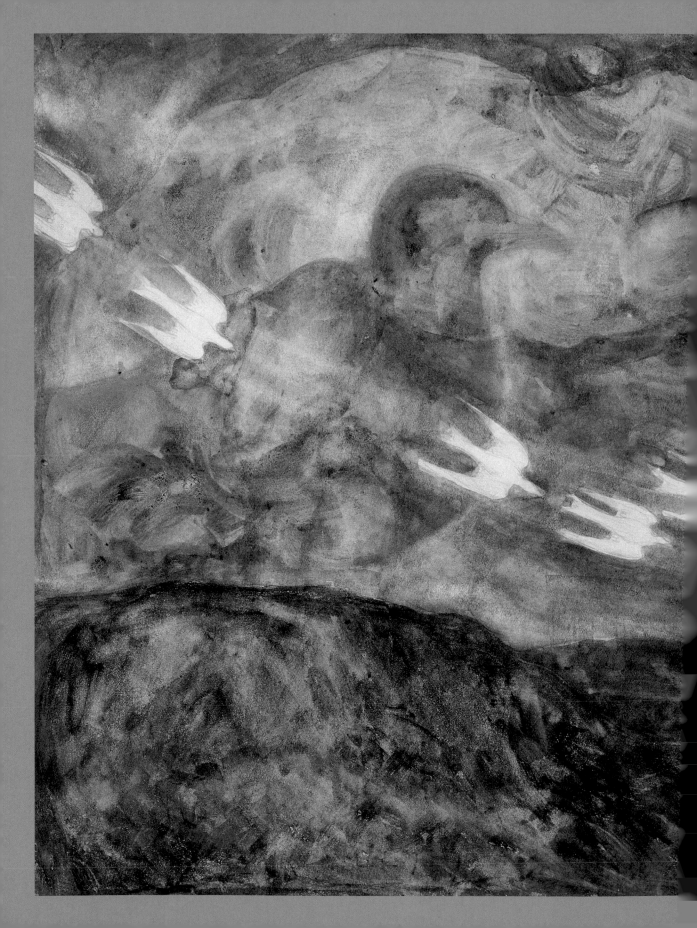

CHAPTER 7

NATURE, SHE
and MAN

Detail from *The Blessed Mountain* (from *Sand and Foam*), c.1926, Watercolor on paper,
8½ x 11 inches (28 x 21.5 cm), The Telfair Museum of Art, Savannah, Georgia

The Great Longing, c.1916, Watercolor and pencil on paper,
8½ x 10⅞ inches (27.6 × 21.6 cm), The Telfair Museum of Art, Savannah, Georgia

The Great Longing

"THIS IS THE LONELIEST song that has been written," Gibran told Mary Haskell as they read the chapter "Of Great Longing" in *Thus Spoke Zarathustra* by the 19th-century German philosopher Friedrich Nietzsche. But then Gibran added, "unless it be what one reads behind the words Christ spoke after the last supper." Among Christ's last words are these moving supplications, "Abba, Father, all things are possible unto thee, take away this cup from me: nevertheless not what I will, but what thou wilt." (Mark 14:36). They read the chapter twice. Gibran was gripped by the profound message about fulfilling one's destiny, even if it remains elusive and enigmatic. Gibran's destiny, or great longing, though Nietzschean in impulse was more optimistic. His message was that the soul of man and the spirit of nature are one with God, who embodies the ultimate longing, desiring all and lifting all toward himself while he seeks ever greater heights. Gibran was so proud of this insight into the evolutionary nature of God that he felt it would transform the history of mankind! The powerfully suggestive "Centaur" series, forty paintings in all, first exhibited in New York then Boston, embody Gibran's evolutionary philosophy. The Centaur is depicted as half-nature half-man, straining toward a higher self.

HERE I SIT between my brother the mountain and my sister the sea.

We three are one in loneliness, and the love that binds us together is deep and strong and strange. Nay, it is deeper than my sister's depth and stronger than my brother's strength, and stranger than the strangeness of my madness.

Æons upon æons have passed since the first gray dawn made us visible to one another; and though we have seen the birth and the fulness and the death of many worlds, we are still eager and young.

We are young and eager and yet we are mateless and unvisited, and though we lie in unbroken half embrace, we are uncomforted. And what comfort is there for controlled desire and unspent passion? Whence shall come the flaming god to warm my sister's bed? And what she-torrent shall quench my brother's fire? And who is the woman that shall command my heart?

In the stillness of the night my sister murmurs in her sleep the fire-god's unknown name, and my brother calls afar upon the cool and distant goddess. But upon whom I call in my sleep I know not.

Here I sit between my brother the mountain and my sister the sea. We three are one in loneliness, and the love that binds us together is deep and strong and strange.

From *The Madman: His Parables and Poems,* 1918

 # Wise Angel!

AND ON A morning when the sun was high, one of the disciples, one of those three who had played with him in childhood, approached him saying: "Master, my garment is worn, and I have no other. Give me leave to go unto the marketplace and bargain that perchance I may procure me new raiment."

And Almustafa looked upon the young man, and he said: "Give me your garment." And he did so and stood naked in the noonday.

And Almustafa said in a voice that was like a young steed running upon a road: "Only the naked live in the sun. Only the artless ride the wind. And he alone who loses his way a thousand times shall have a homecoming.

"The angels are tired of the clever. And it was but yesterday that an angel said to me: 'We created hell for those who glitter. What else but fire can erase a shining surface and melt a thing to its core?'

"And I said: 'But in creating hell you created devils to govern hell.' But the angel answered: 'Nay, hell is governed by those who do not yield to fire.'

"Wise angel! He knows the ways of men and the ways of half-men. He is one of the seraphim who come to minister unto the prophets when they are tempted by the clever. And no doubt he smiled when the prophets smile, and weeps also when they weep.

"My friends and my mariners, only the naked live in the sun. Only the rudderless can sail the greater sea. Only he who is dark with the night shall wake with the dawn, and only he who sleeps with the roots under the snow shall reach the spring.

"For you are even like roots, and like roots are you simple, yet you have wisdom from the earth. And you are silent, yet you have within your unborn branches the choir of the four winds.

"You are frail and you are formless, yet you are the beginning of giant oaks, and of the half-penciled patterned of the willows against the sky.

"Once more I say, you are but roots betwixt the dark sod and the moving heavens. And oftentimes have I seen you rising to dance with the light, but I have also seen you shy. All roots are shy. They have hidden their hearts so long that they know not what to do with their hearts.

"But May shall come, and May is a restless virgin, and she shall mother the hills and plains."

From *The Garden of the Prophet,* 1933

UNLIKE THE 18th-century Swiss philosopher Jean-Jacques Rousseau, Gibran never exactly called for a return to a state of nature—to primitive man. Rather, he believed that we are all primitive in relation to the god-like self that awaits us. As the Wise Angel counsels, Hell is the condition in which we imprison ourselves if we refuse to grow and change. Because for Gibran nature embodied and mirrored the forces of life at work within us, in his art he favored the nude. "I always draw the bodies naked because life is naked," he explained. "If I draw a mountain as a heap of human forms or paint a waterfall in the shape of tumbling human bodies, it is because I see in the mountain a heap of living things, and in the waterfall a precipitate current of life." In 1919, Gibran published Twenty Drawings, which featured "The Mountain," "The Rock" and "The Waterfall." In her introduction to the volume, Alice Raphael praised Gibran's mastery of symbolism and placed him at the crossroads of East and West, in the tradition of the true symbolist who "moves in a world freed from traditions and confines" and for whom "life is a perpetual creation." This is the state of "Primitives" in her view; in Gibran's it is the state of mankind.

Lament of the Field

THE STRIKING CONTRAST between urban life in Boston and New York and the majestic beauty of Gibran's native Bisharri in his Lebanese homeland affected him strongly. Bisharri is a beautiful village perched on a small plateau on one of the cliffs dominating the Valley of Qadisha, and Gibran never tired of drawing on his childhood memories of the place —the serenity of the mountains and the valleys, the mystical beauty of the magnificent cedar trees— and the biblical lore rooted in the landscape. By drawing or daydreaming, he often retreated to these beautiful natural scenes in search of refuge or solace from troubles at home. In *The Processions* (1919), Gibran celebrates such scenes through the voice of a naked youth emerging from the forest, flute in hand. The youth sings of the goodness, beauty and oneness of life in the woods. The long poem is composed using an antiphonal structure in which one voice sings and another responds, with a different rhyme and meter assigned to each. This style was rather innovative in Arabic poetry. The other voice in this poem is of an older man. Representing civilization, he is more jaded and philosophical than the youth. The two voices are in essence two aspects of a divided self contemplating different views of life.

AT THE HOUR of dawn, and just as the sun was about to rise from beyond the horizon, I sat in the middle of a field communing with Nature. At that hour filled with purity and beauty, I lay there in the grass, while men lay in the many folds of slumber, lifted once by a visiting dream and again by a sudden wakefulness. I lay there probing all that my eyes lay upon about the Truth of Beauty, drawing from what were visible articulations of the Beauty of Truth.

And when my reflections began to set me apart from the things of the flesh, and my imaginings began to remove the remaining blotches of matter from my inner self, I began to feel the jolt in my spirit bringing me closer to Nature; unlocking its secrets to me and helping me to understand the language of its creation.

As I was thus absorbed, a breeze passed through the branches, emitting sighs as desperate as those of an orphan who has lost all hope. Astonished, I turned to it asking, seeking to understand: "Why such sighs, gentle breeze?" And it answered: "Because I'm going in the direction of the city, forced thither by the heat of the sun to the city where my pure trails will catch the germs of diseases and the poisoned breath of men will latch on to me. It is for this that you behold sadness in me."

I then turned to the flowers, only to see them shedding their dewdrops like tears, so I asked: "Why the crying of tears, fair flowers?" And one of them lifted its fair head in reply and said: "We cry our tears because man will come and sever our heads and take us to the city to sell us, who are free, like slaves in the marketplace. And when we wither as the evening approaches, he will cast us into the dirt. How do we then not weep when the cruel hand of man will exile us from our home the field?"

And after a while I heard the brook lament like a bereaved mother over her lost ones, so I asked: "Why lament you thus, sweet brook?" He answered me: "Because against my will I am forced to run to the city, wherein man despises me, going rather for the juices of the winepress, and uses me for carrying his dregs. How do I then not bewail when my clarity is about to be muddled and my purity defiled?"

I then hearkened and heard the birds sing a song so sad I thought they were wailing, so I asked them: "Why thus wail, fair birds?" A sparrow then approached and perched on the tip of a nearby branch and said: "A son of Adam is on his way bearing a devilish contraption that will wipe us out as easily as the sickle takes to the standing plant. We are all bidding each other farewell, for we know not who among us will escape the pending doom. How do we not wail when death follows us wherever we turn?"

The sun finally rose from beyond the mountaintop, covering the treetops in wreaths of gold, the while I asked myself: "Why does man destroy that which Nature has builded up?"

From *A Tear and a Smile,* 1914 (trans. Ayman A. El-Desouky)

O Wind

THIS IS GIBRAN'S HYMN to the Holy Spirit, which he believed touches all. The wind invisible is a profound Romantic symbol for the omnipresent, benevolent spirit. It is there as destroyer and preserver of life and a symbol of hope overcoming despair in the English poet Percy Bysshe Shelley's "Ode to the West Wind." Written in 1820, this was most influential on Gibran and later Romantic poets. Just as Gibran was drawn not to the meek Jesus but to Jesus "the mighty hunter" and "the raging tempest," he felt more profoundly moved by August winds than balmy breezes. The Hermit in *The Tempests* (1920) delivers an equally passionate homily on the storm in which it emerges as an awakening force descending on man's conscience. Gibran felt the creative impulse most keenly when it took him "by storm," exposing his thoughts and emotions and clearing away petty cares. Then he could write in the same spirit, hoping to inspire equal strength in his readers. After a particularly creative week, Gibran wrote to Mary Haskell on 8 March 1914, "There was a storm in my being; and I worked night and day, painting, writing, dictating and loving God... There are times when I feel as though I am carried by his great winds to meet the Lord in the sky."

You BLOW, now joyous and swaying, now sighing and bewailing!

We hear but do not see; we feel but do not behold!

You were a sea of love that overtakes our spirits but does not drown them, toying with our hearts even as they remain in steadfastness!

You ascend following the heights and descend to the valleys and spread out over the plains and the meadows.

The strength of will is in your ascent, and gentleness in your descent, and sprightly you spread across.

You were a merciful sovereign, simple and forgiving with the weakling and the fallible mighty and formidable among the powerful and the proud!

In autumn, you roam the valleys wailing, and the trees respond and weep when they hear you;

In winter, you rage, and all of nature rages with you;

In spring, you ail and weaken, and in your weakness there awake the fields;

In summer, you withdraw behind a veil of stillness, and we think you perished, shot by the arrows of the sun, and lain in shrouds of heat.

Did you then as you did, bewail the passing days of autumn? Or mayhap you were mocking the shamed trees as they stood bared at your hands?

And in the days of winter, were you enraged or were you dancing over the graves of snow-thickened nights?

Was it ailment during spring, or were you the pining lover, sickened with separation, and come to caress with her sighs the face of her beloved youth of the seasons, rousing him from his slumber?

Centaur and Child, 1916, Wash drawing, 11 x 8½ inches (21.5 x 28 cm),
Gibran Museum, Bisharri, Lebanon

Did you really perish in summer? Or were you lurking in the core of a fruit and among the grape clusters and on the threshing floors?

From city streets you gather unto you the breath of the sickly, just as you gather unto you the spirits of flowers from the hills!

In like manner do the great spirits, bearing the pains of life, and in like serenity, meet its joys!

You whisper wondrous secrets in the rose's ear. She understands! For she shivers and after she smiles, and so do the gods to the spirits of mortals!

You tarry hither, you hasten and thither you gallop, and cease not! Such too is the essence of man, for it lives in motion and will die if arrested!

On the face of the lake you compose your verses, only to erase them again! As it is so for the genius of poets who come upon the muse repeatedly!

And in wrath you blow over the desert, cruelly trampling the caravans, burying all in graves of sand, layer upon layer.

Are you really then that hidden flood of abundance, doubly then triply masquerading with the colored waves at dawn, iridescent among the leaves on their branches, and stealthily flowing round the turns in the valley?

How then do the flowering plants begin to sway in passionate trances under your spell, and the yellowing stalks embrace feverishly, drunken in the caresses of your breath?

And you rage over the seas, disquieting the stillness of their depths, and when they spew their foaming waves in rebellious fury, you cleft the heights and feed them with ships and men, one forced upon another in bitter morsels!

Are you really then that gentle lover, melting for all, playing tenderly with the fresh locks of children as they run about the homestead?

Whither hasten you thus with our spirits, our sighs, our breaths? Whither carry you forth the traces of our smiles? What do you with the flying sparks of our hearts?

Are you carrying them all yonder, beyond the coloring twilight, beyond this life?

Or mayhap dragging all like prey to distant caverns and frightful caves, where you toss them right and left till they have faded away and vanished?

In the stillness of night, hearts pour out their secrets to you, and at dawn eyes fill you with the flutter of their lids!

Are you then the bearer of memories, all that those hearts have felt and all what the eyes have seen?

In the spread of your heartening wings do the poor entrust their echoes of the crushing burden, the orphan his burning anguish, the sad woman her bitter sighs?

And in the embracing folds of your garbs, does the exiled entrust his longing, and the abandoned the release of his dismay, and the fallen woman her spirit wailings?

Are you then the keeper of the trust of these children of life?

Or like the earth, are you wont to absorb all we entrust to her into her own body?

Hearken you unto this appeal? This howl? These loud cries? This weeping?

Or like the mighty among men do you turn away from stretched hands, and turn your closed ears away from the voices beseeching them in their heights?

Hearken you, O Life of Him that Hears?

From *A Tear and a Smile,* 1914 (trans. Ayman A. El-Desouky)

Detail from *The Rock*, 1916, Wash drawing, 11 x 8¼ inches (21 x 28 cm),
Gibran Museum, Bisharri, Lebanon

 # On Nature

Trees are poems that the earth writes upon the sky.
We fell them down and turn them into paper that we may
record our emptiness.

Should nature heed what we say of contentment no river
would seek the sea, and no winter would turn to Spring.
Should she heed all we say of thrift, how many of us would
be breathing this air?

Strife in nature is but disorder longing for order.

How narrow is the vision that exalts the busyness of the ant
above the singing of the grasshopper.

Said a hunted fox followed by twenty horsemen and a pack of
twenty hounds, "Of course they will kill me. But how poor and
how stupid they must be. Surely it would not be worth while for
twenty foxes riding on twenty asses and accompanied by twenty
wolves to chase and kill one man."

From *Sand and Foam*, 1926

The Hymn of Man

"YOU WERE among the dead and He raised you.
And He shall cause you to die once more,
And after shall He make you to live again,
And unto Him shall ye return." *The Holy Qur'an*

I WAS, from before time!
And, behold me now, I AM!
And I SHALL BE till the end of time!
And my being shall be without end!

I have traversed the expanses of eternities.
I have soared in the worlds of the imagination.
I have come nigh within the circle of higher light.
And now, behold me, a prisoner of matter!

I have hearkened unto the teachings of Confucius.
I listened enraptured in the presence of Brahma's wisdom.
I have sat next to the Buddha under the Tree of
    Knowledge.
And now, behold me, fighting to overcome ignorance and
    unbelieving denial!

I was on the Mount of Sinai as YAHWEH revealed
    himself to Moses.
I crossed the Jordan and witnessed the miracles of the
    Nazarene.
I hearkened to the sayings of the Prophet of the Arabs
    in Medina.
And now, behold me, a prisoner of perplexities!

I beheld the might of Babylon.
I beheld the glory of Egypt.
I beheld the greatness of Greece.

And now do I behold still in all their works poverty,
immateriality, lack of consequence!

I have kept the company of the magicians of Endon.
I have befriended the priests of Assure.
I have followed the prophets of Palestine.
And now do I still seek after the truth!

I have recorded the wisdom revealed in the lands of India.
I have committed to memory the poetry springing in the
    hearts of the Arabians.
I have embraced the music embodying the emotions of
    the Westerners.
And now, behold me, still the unseeing, the unhearing!

I have borne the harshness of unbridled conquerors.
I have suffered the oppression of tyrants.
I have endured the bondage of repressive force.
And now, behold me, still standing, battling with the days!

All this and more have I heard and seen, but the
    fledgling child!
And now in truth shall I hear and see the deeds of youth.
And I shall grow old and reach perfection.
And unto God shall I be returning!

I WAS, from before time!
And, behold me now, I AM!
And I SHALL BE till the end of time!
And my being shall be without end!

From *A Tear and a Smile*, 1914 (trans. Ayman A. El-Desouky)

THE DUALITIES in Gibran's life include the opposing ideas of man and myth. The life he must endure in the present is held up against the possibility of the future, when the higher poet-prophet would emerge from the lower man. These ideas are central to Gibran's personality as well as to his writings. "There's something big in me and I can't get it out," Gibran wrote to Mary Haskell while in the throes of writing *The Prophet* (1923). "It's a silent greater self, sitting and watching a smaller me do all sorts of things. All the things I do seem false to me; they are not what I want to say. I am always conscious of a birth that is to be. It's just as if for years a child wanted to be born and couldn't be born. You are always waiting, and you are always in birth pain." Throughout his life Gibran wished to write about God, the earth and the soul of man, and he was forever searching for the right voice and the appropriate expression. This quest, when eventually fulfilled in the voice of the Prophet, would not only confirm the worth of his life, he felt, but the mediation of his words and vision would help humanity to march toward God.

Nude Figures Lying at the Foot of a Mountain by a Lake, 1920–1923, Watercolor,
11 x 8½ inches (21.5 x 28 cm), Gibran Museum, Bisharri, Lebanon

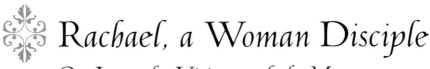

Rachael, a Woman Disciple
On Jesus the Vision and the Man

GIBRAN'S JESUS was his Superman, as he called him. Gibran would often dream that he and Jesus met back in Bisharri. In these dreams, Jesus's humanity became more manifest. "The walnuts and weeping willows arched over the road, and I could see the patches of sunlight falling through on his face," Gibran explained before going on to describe the face he always saw. Mary Haskell recorded it in her Journal on 10 January 1914: "an Arabic type of face, aquiline nose, black, black eyes, deepest and large, yet not weak as large eyes are so apt to be, but as masculine as anything could be, with his straight black brows. His skin was brown and healthy, with that beautiful slight flush of red showing through." Mary would ask whether Jesus had a beard and Gibran would answer "yes." Mary's Journal records many instances when Gibran remarks on his relationship with Jesus and the recurring face. The features are always clearly Middle Eastern, with a bare head, abundant black hair and large, penetrating eyes. Gibran never forgot that face. It became the subject of many drawings of his Superman Jesus and also formed the basis of other faces, like that of John of the Gospels and even the famous image of Almustafa, used as the frontispiece of *The Prophet* (see page 192).

I OFTEN WONDER whether Jesus was a man of flesh and blood like ourselves, or a thought without a body, in the mind, or an idea that visits the vision of man.

Often it seems to me that He was but a dream dreamed by countless men and women at the same time in a sleep deeper than sleep and a dawn more serene than all dawns.

And it seems that in relating the dream, the one to the other, we began to deem it a reality that had indeed come to pass; and in giving it body of our fancy and a voice of our longing we made it a substance of our own substance.

But in truth He was not a dream. We knew Him for three years and beheld Him with our open eyes in the high tide of noon.

We touched His hands, and we followed Him from one place to another. We heard His discourses and witnessed His deeds. Think you that we were a thought seeking after more thought, or a dream in the region of dreams?

Great events always seem alien to our daily lives, though their nature may be rooted in our nature. But though they appear sudden in their coming and sudden in their passing, their true span is for years and for generations.

Jesus of Nazareth was Himself the Great Event. That man whose father and mother and brothers we know, was Himself a miracle wrought in Judea. Yea, all His own miracles, if placed at His feet, would not rise to the height of His ankles.

And all the rivers of all the years shall not carry away our remembrance of Him.

He was a mountain burning in the night, yet He was a soft glow beyond the hills. He was a tempest in the sky, yet He was a murmur in the mist of daybreak.

He was a torrent pouring from the heights to the plains to destroy all things in its path. And He was like the laughter of children.

Every year I had waited for spring to visit this valley. I had waited for the lilies and the cyclamen, and then every year my soul had been saddened within me; for ever I longed to rejoice with the spring, yet I could not.

But when Jesus came to my seasons He was indeed a spring, and in Him was the promise of all the years to come. He filled my heart with joy; and like the violets I grew, a shy thing, in the light of His coming.

And now the changing seasons of worlds not yet ours shall not erase His loveliness from this our world.

Nay, Jesus was not a phantom, nor a conception of the poets. He was man like yourself and myself. But only to sight and touch and hearing; in all other ways He was unlike us.

He was a man of joy; and it was upon the path of joy that He met the sorrows of all men. And it was from the high roofs of His sorrows that He beheld the joy of all men.

He saw visions that we did not see, and heard voices that we did not hear; and He spoke as if to invisible multitudes, and ofttimes He spoke through us to races yet unborn.

And Jesus was often alone. He was among us yet not one with us. He was upon the earth, yet He was of the sky. And only in our aloneness may we visit the land of His aloneness.

He loved us with tender love. His heart was a winepress. You and I could approach with a cup and drink therefrom.

One thing I did not use to understand in Jesus: He would make merry with His listeners; He would tell jests and play upon words, and laugh with all the fullness of His heart, even when there were distances in His eyes and sadness in His voice. But I understand now.

I often think of the earth as a woman heavy with her first child. When Jesus was born, He was the first child. And when He died, He was the first man to die.

For did it not appear to you that the earth was stilled on that dark Friday, and the heavens were at war with the heavens?

And felt you not when His face disappeared from our sight as if we were naught but memories in the mist?

From *Jesus, the Son of Man,* 1928

CHAPTER 8

SELF *and* GREATER SELF

Detail from *The Waterfall*, 1919, (published in *Twenty Drawings*, 1919), Wash drawing,
8¾ x 10¼ inches (26 x 22 cm), Gibran Museum, Bisharri, Lebanon

# On the Greater Self

When you long for blessings that you may not name,
and when you grieve knowing not the cause, then indeed
you are growing with all things that grow, and rising
toward your greater self.

I have never agreed with my other self wholly.
The truth of the matter seems to lie between us.

Your other self is always sorry for you. But your other self
grows on sorrow; so all is well.

You are but a fragment of your giant self, a mouth that seeks
bread, and a blind hand that holds the cup
for a thirsty mouth.

They say to me, "Should you know yourself
you would know all men."
And I say, "Only when I seek all men shall I know myself."

From *Sand and Foam*, 1926

 # Crucified

WHILE IN PARIS in 1909, Gibran wrote to Mary Haskell stating that he wished to portray the life of Jesus as no one had done before. Not long after he wrote in "The Crucified" (published in *The Madman*, 1918), "For centuries Humanity has been worshipping weakness in the person of the Savior. The Nazarene was not weak! He was strong and is strong! But the people refuse to heed the true meaning of strength... Jesus was not a bird with broken wings. He was a raging tempest who broke all crooked wings... Free and brave and daring He was." Not until the 1920s would Gibran devote himself to a work on Christ, *Jesus, the Son of Man* (1928). Here, Gibran explored Jesus's humanity through contemporary and fictionalized accounts. The way in which his character the Madman understands the crucifixion is perhaps the key insight: he places Jesus in Gibran's humanist evolutionary cosmology as a mirror of an evolving God—the ever onward-marching greater self. Gibran explored the vision further in two posthumously published plays, *Lazarus and His Beloved* and *The Blind* (1981). In both, the Madman is again the mouthpiece, unperceived by the plays' characters. The figures of Yuhanna the Madman in *Nymphs of the Valley* (1906) and Khalil the Heretic in *Spirits Rebellious* (1908) are both also clearly Jesus-like.

I CRIED TO MEN, "I would be crucified!"

And they said, "Why should your blood be upon our heads?"

And I answered, "How else shall you be exalted except by crucifying madmen?"

And they heeded and I was crucified. And the crucifixion appeased me.

And when I was hanged between earth and heaven they lifted up their heads to see me. And they were exalted, for their heads had never before been lifted.

But as they stood looking up at me one called out, "For what art thou seeking to atone?"

And another cried, "In what cause dost thou sacrifice thyself?"

And a third said, "Thinkest thou with this price to buy world glory?"

Then said a fourth, "Behold, how he smiles! Can such pain be forgiven?"

And I answered them all, and said:

"Remember only that I smiled. I do not atone—nor sacrifice—nor wish for glory; and I have nothing to forgive. I thirsted—and I besought you to give me my blood to drink. For what is there can quench a madman's thirst but his own blood? I was dumb—and I asked wounds of you for mouths. I was imprisoned in your days and nights—and I sought a door into larger days and nights.

And now I go—as others already crucified have gone. And think not we are weary of crucifixion. For we must be crucified by larger and yet larger men, between greater earths and greater heavens."

From *The Madman: His Parables and Poems,* 1918

The Seven Selves

IN THE STILLEST hour of the night, as I lay half asleep, my seven selves sat together and thus conversed in whispers:

First Self: Here, in this madman, I have dwelt all these years, with naught to do but renew his pain by day and recreate his sorrow by night. I can bear my fate no longer, and now I rebel.

Second Self: Yours is a better lot than mine, brother, for it is given me to be this madman's joyous self. I laugh his laughter and sing his happy hours, and with thrice winged feet I dance his brighter thoughts. It is I that would rebel against my weary existence.

Third Self: And what of me, the love-ridden self, the flaming brand of wild passion and fantastic desires? It is I the love-sick self who would rebel against this madman.

Fourth Self: I, among you all, am the most miserable, for naught was given me but odious hatred and destructive loathing. It is I, the tempest-like self, the one born in the black caves of Hell, who would protest against serving this madman.

Fifth Self: Nay, it is I, the thinking self, the fanciful self, the self of hunger and thirst, the one doomed to wander without rest in search of unknown things and things not yet created; it is I, not you, who would rebel.

Sixth Self: And I, the working self, the pitiful laborer, who, with patient hands, and longing eyes, fashion the days into images and give the formless elements new and eternal forms—it is I, the solitary one, who would rebel against this restless madman.

Seventh Self: How strange that you all would rebel against this man, because each and every one of you has

IN 1913, GIBRAN met the French philosopher Henri Bergson in New York and asked to include his portrait in his "Temple of Art" series (see page 27). Bergson promised to pose for him in Paris. Bergson's philosophy, set out in his 1911 book *Creative Evolution*, explored real change in time alongside the mutation of successive selves, and influenced Marcel Proust's novel *Remembrance of Things Past*, published through the 1920s. Gibran drew on Bergson's ideas, too. In the parable "The Grave-Digger" in *The Madman* (1918) he wrote, "Once, as I was burying one of my dead selves, the gravedigger came by and said to me, 'Of all those who come here to bury, you alone I like.' Said I, 'You please me exceedingly, but why do you like me?' 'Because,' said he, 'they come weeping and go weeping— you only come laughing and go laughing.'" The 1920s saw Gibran's earlier conception—of a fragmented, self redeemed by the greater self—transforming into the idea that to know oneself is to know all people. In his last Arabic work, the play *Iram, City of Lofty Pillars* (included in *Best Things and Masterpieces*, 1923), he stated, "In one atom are found all the elements of the earth;...in one aspect of you are found all the aspects of existence."

a preordained fate to fulfil. Ah! could I but be like one of you, a self with a determined lot! But I have none, I am the do-nothing self, the one who sits in the dumb, empty nowhere and nowhen, while you are busy recreating life. Is it you or I, neighbors, who should rebel?

When the seventh self thus spake the other six selves looked with pity upon him but said nothing more; and as the night grew deeper one after the other went to sleep enfolded with a new and happy submission.

But the seventh self remained watching and gazing at nothingness, which is behind all things.

From *The Madman: His Parables and Poems*, 1918

The Greater Sea

MY SOUL AND I went to the great sea to bathe. And when we reached the shore, we went about looking for a hidden and lonely place.

But as we walked, we saw a man sitting on a grey rock taking pinches of salt from a bag and throwing them into the sea.

"This is the pessimist," said my soul. "Let us leave this place. We cannot bathe here."

We walked on until we reached an inlet. There we saw, standing on a white rock, a man holding a bejeweled box, from which he took sugar and threw it into the sea.

"And this is the optimist," said my soul. "And he too must not see our naked bodies."

Further on we walked. And on a beach we saw a man picking up dead fish and tenderly putting them back into the water.

"And we cannot bathe before him," said my soul. "He is the humane philanthropist."

And we passed on.

Then we came where we saw a man tracing his shadow on the sand. Great waves came and erased it. But he went on tracing it again and again.

"He is the mystic," said my soul. "Let us leave him."

And we walked on, till in a quiet cove we saw a man scooping up the foam and putting it into an alabaster bowl.

"He is the idealist," said my soul. "Surely he must not see our nudity."

And on we walked. Suddenly we heard a voice crying, "This is the sea. This is the deep sea. This is the vast and mighty sea." And when we reached the voice it

THE OCEAN IN Gibran's work invariably stands for God the boundless self, and the rhythm of the sea for the soul's experiences in seeking its own depths. In 1934, Gibran confided in Mikhail Naimy, "Now do I know that I, as an individual, was formed of the same elements as the whole race. Their clay is my clay, their soul is my soul, their inclinations and their goal as my inclinations and my goal." These statements exemplify the force of Gibran's parables. He felt a natural affinity with this ancient Near Eastern form of expression, which draws on aspects of everyday life and natural processes while imparting a universal spiritual message directly to the reader. Gibran's parable on distances in *The Garden of the Prophet* (1933) is itself the best explanation of how he felt toward his readers, "Know you not that there is no distance save that which the soul does not span in fancy? And when the soul shall span the distance, it becomes a rhythm in the soul." This rhythm describes the spiritual evolution that unites us to nature and God and synchronizes our movements, which is why the voice in Gibran's parables seems knowing, authoritative and kindly— especially in his later writings in the 1920s, beginning with *The Prophet* and *The Wanderer*.

was a man whose back was turned to the sea, and at his ear he held a shell, listening to its murmur.

And my soul said, "Let us pass on. He is the realist, who turns his back on the whole he cannot grasp, and busies himself with a fragment."

So we passed on. And in a weedy place among the rocks was a man with his head buried in the sand. And I said to my soul, "We can bathe here, for he cannot see us."

"Nay," said my soul, "For he is the most deadly of them all. He is the puritan."

Then a great sadness came over the face of my soul, and into her voice.

"Let us go hence," she said, "for there is no lonely, hidden place where we can bathe. I would not have this wind lift my golden hair, or bare my white bosom in this air, or let the light disclose my scared nakedness."

Then we left that sea to seek the Greater Sea.

From *The Madman: His Parables and Poems,* 1918

Spiritual Purification and Cosmic Temple, 1923–1926, Watercolor,
10¾ x 14 inches (35.5 x 27.5 cm), Gibran Museum, Bisharri, Lebanon

Purified Humanity Rising Towards the Infinite, 1923–1926, Watercolor,
10 x 14 inches (35.5 x 25.5 cm), Gibran Museum, Bisharri, Lebanon

John the Beloved Disciple
On Jesus the Word

Y OU WOULD HAVE me speak of Jesus, but how can I lure the passion-song of the world into a hollowed reed?

In every aspect of the day Jesus was aware of the Father. He beheld Him in the clouds and in the shadows of the clouds that pass over the earth. He saw the Father's face reflected in the quiet pools, and the faint print of His feet upon the sand; and He often closed His eyes to gaze into the Holy Eyes.

The night spoke to Him with the voice of the Father, and in solitude He heard the angel of the Lord calling to Him. And when He stilled Himself to sleep He heard the whispering of the heavens in His dreams.

He was often happy with us, and He would call us brothers.

Behold, He who was the first Word called us brothers, though we were but syllables uttered yesterday.

You ask why I call Him the first Word.

Listen, and I will answer:

In the beginning God moved in space, and out of His measureless stirring the earth was born and the seasons thereof.

Then God moved again, and life streamed forth, and the longing of life sought the height and the depth and would have more of itself.

Then God spoke, and His words were man, and man was a spirit begotten by God's Spirit.

And when God spoke thus, the Christ was His first Word and that Word was perfect; and when Jesus of Nazareth came to the world the first Word was uttered unto us and the sound was made flesh and blood.

Jesus the Anointed was the first Word of God uttered unto man, even as if an apple tree in an orchard should bud and blossom a day before the other trees. And in God's orchard that day was an æon.

We are all sons and daughters of the Most High, but the Anointed One was His first-born, who dwelt in the body of Jesus of Nazareth, and He walked among us and we beheld Him.

All this I say that you may understand not only in the mind but rather in the spirit. The mind weighs and measures but it is the spirit that reaches the heart of life and embraces the secret; and the seed of the spirit is deathless.

The wind may blow and then cease, and the sea shall swell and then weary, but the heart of life is a sphere quiet and serene, and the star that shines therein is fixed for evermore.

From *Jesus, the Son of Man*, 1928

"CHRIST'S DEATH AS well as his life had a wonderful effect on his followers," Gibran informed Mary Haskell on 6 January 1918. "The day will come when we shall think but just of the Flame—of the fullness of Life that burned in him. Socrates and his followers' relation was more mental, but Christ's followers felt him more than they felt any of his ideas." Gibran held up the example of Jesus not only as a supreme teacher but as the archetype of a man fully connected with his greater, or god-like, self. Jesus taught that the Kingdom of Heaven is within us all—and Gibran believed that this was the greatest of his lessons. He expressed this in his own writings by describing the immanence of the divine in man. Gibran had grown up in the shadow of the Catholic Maronite Church of Lebanon, but his views subsequently became rather unorthodox. Away from the influence of his childhood belief system, he formulated his religious ideas by drawing on a range of Christian, Islamic, mystical and agnostic traditions. Heavily anticlerical, Gibran came to believe in an ideal unity of all the religions, as well as in reincarnation. On the whole he held a rather pantheistic view of the world.

CHAPTER 9

FORERUNNERS
of CREATION

Detail from *William Butler Yeats*, 1911, Charcoal, 17 x 19¾ inches (50 x 43 cm),
Gibran Museum, Bisharri, Lebanon

The Forerunner

"MINE OWN FORERUNNER am I among this people; mine own cockcrow in dark lanes" were not Kahlil Gibran's words, but spoken by Friedrich Nietzsche's Zarathustra (see page 145). Gibran discovered them in Paris between 1908 and 1910, and they were to shape his imagination and sensibilities. The first character to embody Gibran's vision was his Poet; after Paris, he started working on the Madman and then the Forerunner. Later in his career would come the Wanderer and then the Shadow. But eventually it was Almustafa in *The Prophet* who fully materialized as the voice of Gibran's most fundamental insights. He was also his most optimistic creation. In 1928, Gibran confided in May Ziadeh, "If I don't depart before I spell and pronounce my word, I will return to say the word which is now hanging like a cloud in the sky of my heart." These words clearly echo Almustafa's last words in *The Garden of the Prophet*. Around the same time Gibran also mournfully confided in May, "my calamity is that the cloud, which is my reality, longs to hear someone say, 'You are not alone in this world but we are two together, and I know who you are.'" As with Nietzsche, Gibran's need to be recognized by a greater self became his all-consuming thought and essential drive.

YOU ARE YOUR own forerunner, and the towers you have builded are but the foundation of your giant-self. And that self too shall be a foundation.

And I too am my own forerunner, for the long shadow stretching before me at sunrise shall gather under my feet at the noon hour. Yet another sunrise shall lay another shadow before me, and that also shall be gathered at another noon.

Always have we been our own forerunners, and always shall we be. And all that we have gathered and shall gather shall be but seeds for fields yet unploughed. We are the fields and the ploughmen, the gatherers and the gathered.

When you were a wandering desire in the mist, I too was there, a wandering desire. Then we sought one another, and out of our eagerness dreams were born. And dreams were time limitless, and dreams were space without measure.

And when you were a silent word upon Life's quivering lips, I too was there, another silent word. Then Life uttered us and we came down the years throbbing with memories of yesterday and with longing for tomorrow, for yesterday was death conquered and tomorrow was birth pursued.

And now we are in God's hands. You are a sun in His right hand and I an earth in His left hand. Yet you are not more, shining, than I, shone upon.

And we, sun and earth, are but the beginning of a greater sun and a greater earth. And always shall we be the beginning.

You are your own forerunner, you the stranger passing by the gate of my garden.
And I too am my own forerunner, though I sit in the shadows of my trees and seem motionless.

From *The Forerunner: His Parables and Poems,* 1920

John the Son of Zebedee
On the Various Appellations of Jesus

GIBRAN'S LONGEST work, *Jesus, the Son of Man*, written between 1926 and 1927, is also the only one written from scratch after *The Prophet*; all the others he had worked on or been reworking since the 1910s. In this work, finally Gibran is able to express his full vision of the humanity of Christ. Gibran felt that this was integral to "the new message to humanity" he had to impart, along with the concept that God, like us, is always evolving. The format of the work is unique: a series of personal tales of Jesus by a range of biblical characters sits side by side with fictional accounts, all emphasizing Christ's humanity. "Christ changed the human mind and for men found a new path," Gibran had explained to Mary Haskell back in 1918. This is the only book in which Gibran actively experimented with the effect a powerful personality has on the lives of men and women and their self-perception. The accounts end with what we presume are Gibran's own views: those of a Man from Lebanon nineteen centuries later. This book, written in a suggestively biblical style, is Gibran's second most popular work after *The Prophet*, and the one that received most favorable reviews upon publication.

YOU HAVE REMARKED that some of us call Jesus *the Christ,* and some *the Word,* and others call Him the *Nazarene,* and still others the *Son of Man.*

I will try to make these names clear in the light that is given me.

The Christ, He who was in the ancient of days, is the flame of God that dwells in the spirit of man. He is the breath of life that visits us, and takes unto Himself a body like our bodies.

He is the will of the Lord.

He is the first Word, which would speak with our voice and live in our ear that we may heed and understand.

And the Word of the Lord our God built a house of flesh and bones, and was man like unto you and myself.

For we could not hear the song of the bodiless wind nor see our greater self walking in the mist.

Many times the Christ has come to the world, and He has walked many lands. And always He has been deemed a stranger and a madman.

Yet the sound of His voice descended never to emptiness, for the memory of man keeps that which his mind takes no care to keep.

This is the Christ, the innermost and the height, who walks with man toward eternity.

Have you not heard of Him at the crossroads of India? And in the land of the Magi, and upon the sands of Egypt?

And here in your North Country your bards of old sang of Prometheus, the fire-bringer, he who was the desire of man fulfilled, the caged hope made free; and Orpheus, who came with a voice and a lyre to quicken the spirit in beast and man.

And know you not of Mithra the king, and of Zoroaster the prophet of the Persians, who woke from man's ancient sleep and stood at the bed of our dreaming?

We ourselves become man anointed when we meet in the Temple Invisible, once every thousand years. Then comes one forth embodied, and at His coming our silence turns to singing.

Yet our ears turn not always to listening nor our eyes to seeing.

Jesus the Nazarene was born and reared like ourselves; His mother and father were like our parents, and He was a man.

But the Christ, the Word, who was in the beginning, the Spirit who would have us live our fuller life, came unto Jesus and was with Him.

And the Spirit was the versed hand of the Lord, and Jesus was the harp.

The Spirit was the psalm, and Jesus was the tune thereof.

And Jesus, the Man of Nazareth, was the host and the mouthpiece of the Christ, who walked with us in the sun and who called us His friends.

In those days the hills of Galilee and her valleys heard naught but His voice. And I was a youth then, and trod in His path and pursued His footprints.

I pursued His footprints and trod in His path, to hear the words of the Christ from the lips of Jesus of Galilee.

Now you would know why some of us call Him the Son of Man.

He Himself desired to be called by that name, for He knew the hunger and the thirst of man, and He beheld man seeking after His greater self.

The Son of Man was Christ the Gracious, who would be with us all.

He was Jesus the Nazarene who would lead all His brothers to the Anointed One, even to the Word which was in the beginning with God.

In my heart dwells Jesus of Galilee, the Man above men, the Poet who makes poets of us all, the Spirit who knocks at our door that we may wake and rise and walk out to meet truth naked and unencumbered.

From *Jesus, the Son of Man,* 1928

Night and the Madman

"I AM LIKE THEE, O, Night, dark and naked; I walk on the flaming path which is above my daydreams, and whenever my foot touches earth a giant oaktree comes forth."

"Nay, thou art not like me, O, Madman, for thou still lookest backward to see how large a footprint thou leavest on the sand."

"I am like thee, O, Night, silent and deep and in the heart of my loneliness lies a Goddess in child-bed; and in him who is being born Heaven touches Hell."

"Nay, thou art not like me, O, Madman, for thou shudderest yet before pain, and the song of the abyss terrifies thee."

"I am like thee, O, Night, wild and terrible; for my ears are crowded with cries of conquered nations and sighs for forgotten lands."

"Nay, thou art not like me, O, Madman, for thou still takest thy little-self for a comrade, and with thy monster-self thou canst not be friend."

"I am like thee, O, Night, cruel and awful; for my bosom is lit by burning ships at sea, and my lips are wet with blood of slain warriors."

"Nay, thou art not like me, O, Madman; for the desire for a sister spirit is yet upon thee, and thou hast not become a law unto thyself."

"I am like thee, O, Night, joyous and glad; for he who dwells in my shadow is now drunk with virgin wine, and she who follows me is sinning mirthfully."

"Nay, thou art not like me, O, Madman, for thy soul is wrapped in the veil of seven folds and thou holdest not thy heart in thine hand."

"I am like thee, O, Night, patient and passionate; for in my breast a thousand dead lovers are buried in shrouds of withered kisses."

"Yea, Madman, art thou like me? Art thou like me? And canst thou ride the tempest as a steed, and grasp the lightning as a sword?"

"Like thee, O, Night, like thee, mighty and high, and my throne is built upon heaps of fallen Gods; and before me too pass the days to kiss the hem of my garment but never to gaze at my face."

"Art thou like me, child of my darkest heart? And dost thou think my untamed thoughts and speak my vast language?"

"Yea, we are twin brothers, O, Night; for thou revealest space and I reveal my soul."

From *The Madman: His Parables and Poems,* 1918

WHEN IT FIRST appeared in October 1918, *The Madman* included as a publicity stunt a statement from the great sculptor Auguste Rodin hailing Kahlil Gibran as "the William Blake of the twentieth century" and stating that "the world should expect more from this poet-painter of Lebanon." The publicity worked, and the work received its fair share of acclaim, with reviews in the American periodicals *The Nation* and *The Dial. The New York Evening Post* published a review favorably comparing Gibran with the Bengali poet Rabindranath Tagore. A year later, Gibran wrote to May Ziadeh, who had detected in the figure of the Madman elements of "cruelty" and "dark caverns," and explained that "the madman is not wholly myself, the thoughts and inclinations I tried to express are by no means a complete picture of my own thoughts and inclinations." But by the time *The Madman* was in print, Gibran had moved on, working on parables that would be published as *The Forerunner.* Over the following two years he was invited to give readings in such illustrious establishments as America's most famous Artists Colony, The MacDowell Colony in Peterborough, New Hampshire, while his paintings were exhibited in Fifth Avenue galleries next to works by Pierre Bonnard, Paul Cézanne, Camille Pissarro and others.

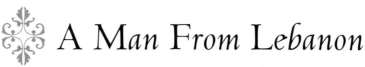

A Man From Lebanon
Nineteen Centuries Afterwards

IN THIS CONCLUDING hymn to Jesus from *Jesus, the Son of Man*, Gibran describes him as the Master Poet and Master Singer whose words reveal man's essential nature and point us on the path to renewal and spiritual elevation. Gibran states that once we recognize this and follow Christ's example, each of us can be our own "creator." In *Sand and Foam* (1928) he described meeting Jesus: "the first time He was asking a policeman not to take a prostitute to prison; the second time He was drinking wine with an outcast; and the third time He was having a fistfight with a promoter inside a church." If we simply proclaim his divinity without following his example, Gibran thought, we lose the potential for positive change. Gibran often mentioned to close friends, especially Mary Haskell and his model Charlotte Teller, that he and Jesus had long conversations in his dreams, both speaking "the most beautiful language," "Chaldeo-Syriac" (Aramaic). He described how Jesus entrusted him with parables that had not found their way into the Gospels. "Jesus lives still—through 2000 years and from 8000 miles away," he told Mary on 22 February 1911, before stating that Jesus was actually born on January 6, his own birthday and the day on which the Armenian Church celebrates Christmas.

Master, master singer
Master of words unspoken,
Seven times was I born, and seven times have I died
Since your hasty visit and our brief welcome.
And behold I live again,
Remembering a day and a night among the hills,
When your tide lifted us up.
Thereafter many lands and many seas did I cross,
And wherever I was led by saddle or sail
Your name was prayer or argument.
Men would bless you or curse you;
The curse, a protest against failure,
The blessing, a hymn of the hunter
Who comes back from the hills
With provision for his mate.

Your friends are yet with us for comfort and support,
And your enemies also, for strength and assurance.
Your mother is with us;
I have beheld the sheen of her face in the countenance
    of all mothers;
Her hand rocks cradles with gentleness,
Her hand folds shrouds with tenderness.
And Mary Magdalen is yet in our midst,
She who drank the vinegar of life, and then its wine.
And Judas, the man of pain and small ambitions,
He too walks the earth;

Even now he preys upon himself when his hunger finds
     naught else,
And seeks his larger self in self-destruction.

And John, he whose youth loved beauty, is here,
And he sings though unheeded.
And Simon Peter the impetuous, who denied you that he might live longer
     for you,
He too sits by our fire.
He may deny you again ere the dawn of another day,
Yet he would be crucified for your purpose, and deem himself unworthy
     of the honor.
And Caiaphas and Annas still live their day,
And judge the guilty and the innocent.
They sleep upon their feathered bed
Whilst he whom they have judged is whipped with the rods.

And the woman who was taken in adultery,
She too walks the streets of our cities,
And hungers for bread not yet baked,
And she is alone in an empty house.
And Pontius Pilatus is here also:
He stands in awe before you,
And still questions you,
But he dares not risk his station or defy an alien race;
And he is still washing his hands.
Even now Jerusalem holds the basin and Rome the ewer,
And betwixt the two a thousand thousand hands would be washed to whiteness.

Master, Master Poet,
Master of words sung and spoken,
They have builded temples to house your name,
And upon every height they have raised your cross,
A sign and a symbol to guide their wayward feet,
But not unto your joy.
Your joy is a hill beyond their vision,
And it does not comfort them.
They would honor the man unknown to them.
And what consolation is there in a man like themselves, a man
    whose kindliness is like their own kindliness,
A god whose love is like their own love,
And whose mercy is in their own mercy?
They honor not the man, the living man,
The first man who opened His eyes and gazed at the sun
With eyelids unquivering.
Nay, they do not know Him, and they would not be like Him.

They would be unknown, walking in the procession of the unknown.
They would bear sorrow, their sorrow,
And they would not find comfort in your joy.
Their aching heart seeks not consolation in your words
    and the song thereof.
And their pain, silent and unshapen,
Makes them creatures lonely and unvisited.
Though hemmed about by kin and kind,
They live in fear, uncomraded;
Yet they would not be alone.
They would bend eastward when the west wind blows.

Detail from *Carl Gustav Jung*, 1913, Charcoal, 17 1/10 x 17 inches (43.2 x 43.5 cm),
Gibran Museum, Bisharri, Lebanon

They call you king,
And they would be in your court.
They pronounce you the Messiah,
And they would themselves be anointed with the holy oil.
Yea, they would live upon your life.

Master, Master Singer,
Your tears were like the showers of May,
And your laughter like the waves of the white sea.
When you spoke your words were the far-off whisper of their lips
    when those lips should be kindled with fire;
You laughed for the marrow in their bones that was not yet ready
    for laughter;
And you wept for their eyes that yet were dry.
Your voice fathered their thoughts and their understanding.
Your voice mothered their words and their breath.

Seven times was I born and seven times have I died,
And now I live again, and I behold you,
The fighter among fighters,
The poet of poets
King above all kings,
A man half naked with your road-fellows.
Every day the bishop bends down his head
When he pronounces your name.
And every day the beggars say:
"For Jesus' sake
Give us a penny to buy bread."

We call upon each other,
But in truth we call upon you,
Like the flood tide in the spring of our want and desire,
And when our autumn comes, like the ebb tide.
High or low, your name is upon our lips,
The Master of infinite compassion.

Master, Master of our lonely hours,
Here and there, betwixt the cradle and the coffin, I meet your silent brothers,
The free men, unshackled,
Sons of your mother earth and space.
They are like the birds of the sky,
And like the lilies of the field.
They live your life and think your thoughts,
And they echo your song.
But they are empty-handed,
And they are not crucified with the great crucifixion,
And therein is their pain.
The world crucifies them every day,
But only in little ways.
The sky is not shaken,
And the earth travails not with her dead.
They are crucified and there is none to witness their agony.
They turn their face to right and left
And find not one to promise them a station in his kingdom.
Yet they would be crucified again and yet again,
That your God may be their God,
And your Father their Father.

Master, Master Lover,
The Princess awaits your coming in her fragrant chamber,
And the married unmarried woman in her cage;
The harlot who seeks bread in the streets of her shame,
And the nun in her cloister who has no husband;
The childless woman too at her window,
Where frost designs the forest on the pane,
She finds you in that symmetry,
And she would mother you, and be comforted.

Master, Master Poet,
Master of our silent desires,
The heart of the world quivers with the throbbing of your heart,
But it burns not with your song.
The world sits listening to your voice in tranquil delight,
But it rises not from its seat
To scale the ridges of your hills.
Man would dream your dream but he would not wake to your dawn
Which is his greater dream.
He would see with your vision,
But he would not drag his heavy feet to your throne.
Yet many have been enthroned in your name
And mitred with your power,
And have turned your golden visit
Into crowns for their head and sceptres for their hand.
Master, Master of Light,
Whose eye dwells in the seeking fingers of the blind,
You are still despised and mocked,

Rabindranath Tagore, 1916, Charcoal, 10½ x 15½ inches (37 x 26.5 cm),
Gibran Museum, Bisharri, Lebanon

Abdul Baha, 1912, Charcoal, 18 x 26½ inches (68 × 45.7 cm) Peter A. Juley & Son Collection, Smithsonian American Art Museum, Washington DC, USA

A man too weak and infirm to be God,
A God too much man to call forth adoration.
Their mass and their hymn,
Their sacrament and their rosary, are for their imprisoned self.
You are their yet distant self, their far-off cry, and their passion.

But Master, Sky-heart, Knight of our fairer dream,
You do still tread this day;
Nor bows nor spears shall stay your steps.
You walk through all our arrows.
You smile down upon us,
And though you are the youngest of us all
You father us all.

Poet, Singer, Great Heart,
May our God bless your name,
And the womb that held you, and the breasts that gave you milk.
And may God forgive us all.

From *Jesus, the Son of Man*, 1928

CHAPTER 10

PROPHET
of MAN

Detail from *Face of Almustafa* (frontispiece for *The Prophet*), 1923, Charcoal,
15½ x 18½ inches (47 x 39.5 cm), Gibran Museum, Bisharri, Lebanon

# The Coming of the Ship

ALMUSTAFA, THE CHOSEN and the beloved, who was a dawn unto his own day, had waited twelve years in the city of Orphalese for his ship that was to return and bear him back to the isle of his birth.

And in the twelfth year, on the seventh day of Ielool, the month of reaping, he climbed the hill without the city walls and looked seaward; and he beheld his ship coming with the mist.

Then the gates of his heart were flung open, and his joy flew far over the sea. And he closed his eyes and prayed in the silences of his soul.

But as he descended the hill, a sadness came upon him, and he thought in his heart:

How shall I go in peace and without sorrow? Nay, not without a wound in the spirit shall I leave this city.

Long were the days of pain I have spent within its walls, and long were the nights of aloneness; and who can depart from his pain and his aloneness without regret?

Too many fragments of the spirit have I scattered in these streets, and too many are the children of my longing that walk naked among these hills, and I cannot withdraw from them without a burden and an ache.

It is not a garment I cast off this day, but a skin that I tear with my own hands.

Nor is it a thought I leave behind me, but a heart made sweet with hunger and with thirst.

Yet I cannot tarry longer.

The sea that calls all things unto her calls me, and I must embark.

For, to stay, though the hours burn in the night, is to freeze and crystallize and be bound in a mold.

Fain would I take with me all that is here. But how shall I?

A voice cannot carry the tongue and the lips that give it wings. Alone must it seek the ether.

And alone and without his nest shall the eagle fly across the sun.

From *The Prophet*, 1923

ALMUSTAFA in *The Prophet* is a composite of Jesus and the Prophet Muhammad (one of the most common appellations for the Prophet is Almustafa, The Chosen One). However, the figure voiced Gibran's own vision. Mikhail Naimy, who alone with Mary Haskell received the typescript of *The Prophet* before publication, offered a penetrating insight into the character when he described Gibran's drawing of Almustafa (one of twelve originals prepared for the book): "the large, dreamy eyes seem to look away beyond the present moment and the immediate circumstance. Sorrowful and penetrating, they speak eloquently of a most sympathetic heart and a soul suffused with loving understanding." The face had haunted Gibran in his dreams, sometimes forcing him to wake up in order to add this or that detail. Almustafa, though clearly a fictive creation of Gibran's, still embodies clearly autobiographical aspects. The twelve years Almustafa has been away are the years Gibran spent in New York up to the writing of the Prelude to *The Prophet*. The City of Orphalese is New York itself, while the Isle of his Birth is Lebanon or the secluded Bisharri. Almitra the priestess is Mary Haskell "who had first sought and believed in him" and the promise of return is the prospect of reincarnation.

Kahlil Gibran, Date unknown, Photographer unknown

On Self-Knowledge

BY THE MID-1920S, Gibran began to identify more confidently with the role of prophet. Though he would shyly deny that he was his own Prophet, he delighted in the many letters arriving from every part of America, and Mary Haskell and others did begin to visit him as a spiritual teacher. *The Prophet...*is my rebirth and my first baptism," he wrote to his beloved May Ziadeh in Cairo on 9 November 1919, "For this prophet had already 'written' me before I attempted to 'write' him, had created me before I created him, and had silently set me on a course to follow him for seven thousand leagues before he appeared in front of me to dictate his wishes and inclinations." Gibran's paintings and writing began to be noticed by some liberal churches, and he was invited to speak before their congregations. But, as his health began to fail and his creative energy to wane, Gibran began to entertain self-doubts about how far he really embodied his own vision of human potential. In a famous episode during a walk with close Arab friends, Mikhail Naimy reports that Gibran suddenly halted, shouting "Mischa! I'm a false alarm!"

AND A MAN said, Speak to us of Self-Knowledge.
And he answered, saying:

Your hearts know in silence the secrets of the days and the nights.

But your ears thirst for the sound of your heart's knowledge.

You would know in words that which you have always known in thought.

You would touch with your fingers the naked body of your dreams.

And it is well you should.

The hidden well-spring of your soul must needs rise and run murmuring to the sea;

And the treasure of your infinite depths would be revealed to your eyes.

But let there be no scales to weigh your unknown treasure;

And seek not the depths of your knowledge with staff or sounding line.

For self is a sea boundless and measureless.

Say not, "I have found the truth," but rather, "I have found a truth."

Say not, "I have found the path of the soul." Say rather, "I have met the soul walking upon my path."

For the soul walks upon all paths.

The soul walks not upon a line, neither does it grow like a reed.

The soul unfolds itself, like a lotus of countless petals.

From *The Prophet,* 1923

It was the Boundless in You!

Know therefore, that from the greater silence I shall return.

The mist that drifts away at dawn, leaving but dew in the fields, shall rise and gather into a cloud and then fall down in rain.

And not unlike the mist have I been.

In the stillness of the night I have walked in your streets, and my spirit has entered your houses,

And your heart-beats were in my heart, and your breath was upon my face, and I knew you all.

Ay, I knew your joy and your pain, and in your sleep your dreams were my dreams.

And oftentimes I was among you a lake among the mountains.

I mirrored the summits in you and the bending slopes, and even the passing flocks of your thoughts and your desires.

And to my silence came the laughter of your children in streams, and the longing of your youths in rivers.

And when they reached my depth the streams and the rivers ceased not yet to sing.

But sweeter still than laughter and greater than longing came to me.

It was the boundless in you;

The vast man in whom you are all but cells and sinews;

He in whose chant all your singing is but a soundless throbbing.

It is in the vast man that you are vast,

And in beholding him that I beheld you and loved you.

For what distances can love reach that are not in that vast sphere?

What visions, what expectations and what presumptions can outsoar that flight?

Like a giant oak tree covered with apple blossoms is the vast man in you.

His might binds you to the earth, his fragrance lifts you into space, and in his durability you are deathless.

You have been told that, even like a chain, you are as weak as your weakest link.

This is but half the truth. You are also as strong as your strongest link.

To measure you by your smallest deed is to reckon the power of ocean by the frailty of its foam.

To judge you by your failures is to cast blame upon the seasons for their inconstancy.

Ay, you are like an ocean,

From *The Prophet*, 1923

THE CHARISMA OF Gibran extended beyond the literary world of lecture circles and reading rooms. One telling anecdote describes Gibran's mesmeric effect on many of those with whom he came into contact, and was told by journalist and playwright Witter Bynner. He introduced Gibran to Alfred Knopf, who eventually published all his works in English. Bynner recalled a dinner at the home of New York socialite and philanthropist Julia Ellsworth Ford: "the maids failed to bring on one of the courses, and after a considerable wait and several bell ringings, Mrs. Ford rose and went to the pantry. There, behind a screen, stood two maids. When reprimanded, one of them explained, 'But Mrs. Ford, how can we go about our business when Mr Gibran is talking? He sounds like Jesus?' And he did." This anecdote echoes the incident in the Gospels with Mary and Martha: Mary chooses to drop the house chores and sit at the feet of Jesus to listen to him, while her sister Martha reprimands her! Almustafa reassures the people of Orphalese that he only gives voice to their silent dreams and innermost desires, and Gibran felt that his calling was to play this role for the common man. This ambition reveals his remarkably human and sympathetic vision and explains the simplicity of his style.

On Teaching

Detail from *The Triad Being Descending Towards the Mother-Sea*, 1923, (illustration for *The Prophet*, 1923), Watercolor, 8½ x 11 inches (28 x 21.5 cm), Gibran Museum, Bisharri, Lebanon

THEN SAID A teacher, Speak to us of Teaching. And he said:

No man can reveal to you aught but that which already lies half asleep in the dawning of your knowledge.

The teacher who walks in the shadow of the temple, among his followers, gives not of his wisdom but rather of his faith and his lovingness.

If he is indeed wise he does not bid you enter the house of wisdom, but rather leads you to the threshold of your own mind.

The astronomer may speak to you of his understanding of space, but he cannot give you his understanding.

The musician may sing to you of the rhythm which is in all space, but he cannot give you the ear which arrests the rhythm nor the voice that echoes it.

And he who is versed in the science of numbers can tell of the regions of weight and measure, but he cannot conduct you thither.

For the vision of one man lends not its wings to another man.

And even as each one of you stands alone in God's knowledge, so must each one of you be alone in his knowledge of God and in his understanding of the earth.

From *The Prophet*, 1923

 # White Silence

AND ONE SAID: "Speak to us of that which is moving in your own heart even now."

And he looked upon that one, and there was in his voice a sound like a star singing, and he said: "In your waking dream, when you are hushed and listening to your deeper self, your thoughts, like snowflakes, fall and flutter and garment all the sounds of your spaces with white silence.

"And what are waking dreams but clouds that bud and blossom on the sky-tree of your heart? And what are your thoughts but the petals which the winds of your heart scatter upon the hills and its fields?

"And even as you wait for peace until the formless within you takes form, so shall the cloud gather and drift until the Blessed Fingers shape its grey desire to little crystal suns and moons and stars."

Then Sarkis, he who was the half-doubter, spoke and said: "But spring shall come, and all the snows of our dreams and our thoughts shall melt and be no more."

And he answered saying: "When Spring comes to seek His beloved among the slumbering groves and vineyards, the snows shall indeed melt and shall run in streams to seek the river in the valley, to be the cup-bearer to the myrtle trees and laurel.

"So shall the snow of your heart melt when your Spring is come, and thus shall your secret run in streams to seek the river of life in the valley. And the river shall enfold your secret and carry it to the great sea.

"All things shall melt and turn into songs when Spring comes. Even the stars, the vast snowflakes that fall slowly upon the larger fields, shall melt into singing

WHENEVER IT SNOWED in New York, Gibran remembered how, back home in his village in the north of Lebanon, he used "to make shapes and figures from the snow, which melted as soon as the sun came up." This became, for Gibran, a metaphor for how we emerge from life-eternal at birth and return to it with our last breath, just as every drop of water eventually rejoins the infinite ocean. Gibran believed in reincarnation and shared this belief with Charlotte Teller and Mary Haskell, occasionally boasting of his past lives: "twice in Syria—short lives only; once in Italy till I was 25; in Greece till 22; in Egypt till an old, old age; several times, maybe six or seven in Chaldea; once in India; and in Persia once—all as a human being. I don't know anything about my lives before then." In response, as Mary recorded in her journals, she and Charlotte speculated that Gibran may have also lived as William Blake and as the Pre-Raphaelite painter Dante Gabriel Rossetti. They made their calculations on the basis that Blake had died in 1827 and Rossetti had been born a year later. Rossetti passed away in 1882, a year before Gibran was born!

streams. When the sun of His face shall rise above the wider horizon, then what frozen symmetry would not turn into liquid melody? And who among you would not be the cupbearer to the myrtle and the laurel?

"It was but yesterday that you were moving with the moving sea, and you were shoreless and without a self. Then the wind, the breath of Life, wove you, a veil of light on her face; then her hand gathered you and gave you form, and with a head held high you sought the heights. But the sea followed after you, and her song is still with you. And though you have forgotten your parentage, she will for ever assert her motherhood, and for ever will she call you unto her.

"In your wanderings among the mountains and the desert you will always remember the depth of her cool heart. And though oftentimes you will not know for what you long, it is indeed for her vast and rhythmic peace.

"And how else can it be? In grove and in bower when the rain dances in leaves upon the hill, when snow falls, a blessing and a covenant; in the valley when you lead your flocks to the river; in your fields where brooks, like silver streams, join together the green garment; in your gardens when the early dews mirror the heavens; in your meadows when the mist of evening half veils your way; in all these the sea is with you, a witness to your heritage, and a claim upon your love.

"It is the snowflake in you running down to the sea."

From *The Garden of the Prophet*, 1933

 # A Homecoming in His Heart

ALMUSTAFA, THE CHOSEN and the beloved, who was a noon unto his own day, returned to the isle of his birth in the month of Tichreen, which is the month of remembrance.

And as his ship approached the harbor, he stood upon its prow, and his mariners were about him. And there was a homecoming in his heart.

And he spoke, and the sea was in his voice, and he said: "Behold, the isle of our birth. Even here the earth heaved us, a song and a riddle; a song unto the sky, a riddle unto the earth; and what is there between earth and sky that shall carry the song and solve the riddle save our own passion?

"The sea yields us once more to these shores. We are but another wave of her waves. She sends us forth to sound her speech, but how shall we do so unless we break the symmetry of our heart on rock and sand?

"For this is the law of mariners and the sea: If you would freedom, you must needs turn to mist. The formless is for ever seeking form, even as the countless nebulæ would become suns and moons; and we who have sought much and return now to this isle, rigid molds, we must become mist once more and learn of the beginning. And what is there that shall live and rise unto the heights except it be broken unto passion and freedom?

"For ever shall we be in quest of the shores, that we may sing and be heard. But what of the wave that breaks where no ear shall hear? It is the unheard in us that nurses our deeper sorrow. Yet it is also the unheard which carves our soul to form and fashions our destiny."

Then one of his mariners came forth and said: "Master, you have captained our longing for this harbor, and behold, we have come. Yet you speak of sorrow, and of hearts that shall be broken."

And he answered him and said: "Did I not speak of freedom, and of the mist which is our greater freedom? Yet it is in pain I make pilgrimage to the isle where I was born, even like unto a ghost of one slain come to kneel before those who have slain him."

From *The Garden of the Prophet*, 1933

RECORDS OF GIBRAN'S conversations with friends and his correspondence are littered with expressions of longing for his native Bisharri and his homeland Lebanon; there was forever "a homecoming in his heart." Gibran would also explain the creative process—the act of rendering his innermost thoughts and visions into words and images —as so many experiences of "homecoming." Barely a year before his death, Gibran wrote to his friend and Arab compatriot Felix Farris, "I must go back to Lebanon, and I must withdraw myself from this civilization that runs on wheels. However, I deem it wise not to leave this country before I break the strings and chains that tie me down; and numerous are those strings and those chains! I wish to go back to Lebanon and remain there forever." Gibran's life is perhaps best understood in terms of transition and transformation, from the 19th century to the 20th century, from the Romantic ideal to the modern, from the constraints of historical tradition to the freedom of the individual imagination, and from East to West, with a whole world of possibilities created by the constant shuttling back and forth. The result is a creative life spent passionately and intimately exploring what it is to be human, and expressing our potential in simple but often radical ways.

And Life is Veiled and Hidden

IN HIS FINAL YEARS, Gibran became increasingly reclusive, battling sickness and almost desperately tugging at the veil of life to tease out from its "hiddenness" the word he wished finally to utter. Still, he managed to meet yet another woman supporter, Barbara Young, whose secretarial skills kept his writing and publishing affairs in order. Barbara had heard Butler Davenport, a New York Pastor, read *The Prophet* in St. Mark's-in-the-Bouwerie and was deeply moved, as was Gibran himself, who had long wished for the book to be read aloud in church. Barbara would transcribe *Jesus, the Son of Man*, prepare *The Garden of the Prophet* for publication after Gibran's death, and publish his first biography, *This Man from Lebanon*. As Gibran became better recognized internationally, he was invited by Syud Hossain to become an officer of The New Orient Society in New York and contribute to its quarterly journal. His status as a figurehead of the Syrian community, especially in Boston, was also confirmed, and though suspicious of social work, which he saw as an intrusion on others' lives, he supported an agency working with Boston's Syrian children and growing Chinese community. On 5 January 1929, Gibran received tributes from the Arab-American community as *Arrabitah*, the Pen Club he had founded, sponsored a testimonial dinner in New York.

And one spoke and said: "Master, life has dealt bitterly with our hopes and our desires. Our hearts are troubled, and we do not understand. I pray you, comfort us, and open to us the meanings of our sorrows."

And his heart was moved with compassion, and he said: "Life is older than all things living; even as beauty was winged ere the beautiful was born on earth, and even as truth was truth ere it was uttered.

"Life sings in our silences, and dreams in our slumber. Even when we are beaten and low, Life is enthroned and high. And when we weep, Life smiles upon the day, and is free even when we drag our chains.

"Oftentimes we call Life bitter names, but only when we ourselves are bitter and dark. And we deem her empty and unprofitable, but only when the soul goes wandering in desolate places, and the heart is drunken with over-mindfulness of self.

"Life is deep and high and distant; and though only your vast vision can reach even her feet, yet she is near; and though only the breath of your breath reaches her heart, the shadow of your shadow crosses her face, and the echo of your faintest cry becomes a spring and an autumn in her breast.

"And Life is veiled and hidden, even as your greater self is hidden and veiled. Yet when Life speaks, all the winds become words; and when she speaks again, the smiles upon your lips and the tears in your eyes turn also into words. When she sings, the deaf hear and are held; and when she comes walking, the sightless behold her and are amazed and follow her in wonder and astonishment."

From *The Garden of the Prophet*, 1933

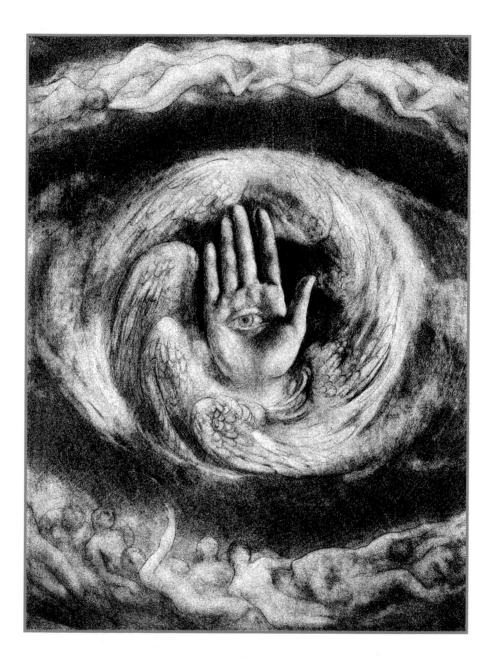

The Divine World, 1923, (illustration for *The Prophet)*, Charcoal, 8½ x 11 inches (28 x 21.6 cm), Gibran Museum, Bisharri, Lebanon

Master Speak to us of Being

And after a space one of the disciples asked him saying: "Master, speak to us of *being*. What is it to *be*?"

And Almustafa looked long upon him and loved him. And he stood up and walked a distance away from them; then returning, he said: "In this Garden my father and my mother lie, buried by the hands of the living; and in this Garden lie buried the seeds of yesteryear, bought hither upon the wings of the wind. A thousand times shall my mother and my father be buried here, and a thousand times shall the wind bury the seed; and a thousand years hence shall you and I and these flowers come together in this Garden even as now, and we shall *be*, loving life, and we shall *be*, dreaming of space, and we shall *be*, rising toward the sun.

"But now today to *be* is to be wise, though not a stranger to the foolish; it is to be strong, but not to the undoing of the weak; to play with young children, not as fathers, but rather as playmates who would learn their games;

"To be simple and guileless with old men and women, and to sit with them in the shade of the ancient oak trees, though you are still walking with Spring;

"To seek a poet though he may live beyond the seven rivers, and to be at peace in his presence, nothing wanting, nothing doubting, and with no question upon your lips;

"To know that the saint and the sinner are twin brothers, whose father is our Gracious King, and that one was born but the moment before the other, wherefore we regard him as the Crowned Prince;

"To follow Beauty even when she shall lead you to the verge of the precipice; and though she is winged and you are wingless, and though she shall pass beyond the verge, follow her, for where Beauty is not, there is nothing;

"To be a garden without walls, a vineyard without a guardian, a treasure-house for ever open to passersby;

"To be robbed, cheated, deceived, ay, misled and trapped and then mocked, yet with it all to look down from the height of your larger self and smile, knowing that there is a spring that will come to your garden to dance in your leaves, and an autumn to ripen your grapes; knowing that if but one of your

THE MESSAGE IN *The Prophet*, Gibran explained to Mary Haskell on 2 January 2 1923, is that "all is well." He said that the message of *The Garden of the Prophet* is that "all is beautiful." Gibran's messages are as simple as accepting that life continues in different forms, akin to the seasons and nature's cycles of life and death. This faith in an eternal life provides hope, helps us to transcend suffering and despair, and encourages the recognition that others share our passions, fears and destiny. Gibran had no metaphysical or systematic theory of existence; his were merely intimations of the world and the human condition. Gibran believed that though we each have our path in life, humanity is a collective enterprise: the fate of one is the fate of all. Some scholars have sought to systematize Gibran's views on existence and human relations into an intuitive or "people's" philosophy. Gibran himself never had the impulse to systematize his thoughts, only to express in the most profound way he could muster the insights he extracted from the world of human affairs. These insights, he felt, issued from a single source, which he envisaged as his deeper or greater self. But because it was always evolving, this self was never fully reachable.

windows is open to the East, you shall never be empty; knowing that all those deemed wrongdoers and robbers, cheaters and deceivers are your brothers in need, and that you are perchance all of these in the eyes of the blessed inhabitants of that City Invisible, above this city.

"And now, to you also whose hands fashion and find all things that are needful for the comfort of our days and our nights—

"To *be* is to be a weaver with seeing fingers, a builder mindful of light and space; to be a ploughman and feel that you are hiding a treasure with every seed you sow; to be a fisherman and a hunter with a pity for the fish and for the beast, yet a still greater pity for the hunger and need of man.

"And, above all, I say this: I would have you each and every one partners to the purpose of every man, for only so shall you hope to obtain your own good purpose.

"My comrades and my beloved, be bold and not meek; be spacious and not confined; and until my final hour and yours be indeed your greater self."

And he ceased from speaking and there fell a deep gloom upon the nine, and their heart was turned away from him, for they understood not his words.

And behold, the three men who were mariners longed for the sea; and they who head served in the Temple yearned for the consolation of her sanctuary; and they who had been his playfellows desired the marketplace. They all were deaf to his words, so that the sound of them returned unto him like weary and homeless birds seeking refuge.

From *The Garden of the Prophet*, 1933

A Rhythm and a Fragrance

WHEN FIRST WRITING in English, Gibran had misgivings about his ability to write in a language other than his native Arabic. But then he had a penetrating insight. He told Mary Haskell on 21 April 1916, "there is absolute language, just as there is absolute form—an expression may be absolute just as a triangle is absolute. People may add this and that—but the eye will perceive in it the triangle. I am always seeking the absolute in language." Mary edited his English and had a hand in many turns of phrase in *The Prophet*, but the language did come, eventually in the form of biblical English rhythms and cadences. He felt these approximated "Chaldeo-Syriac," the language he claimed to share with Jesus. As to the form of his "Counsels," as he referred to the sections of *The Prophet*, he decided with Mary that the Book of Job made a good model, in its brevity and its line and section division. He said, "Poets ought to listen to the rhythm of the sea. That's the rhythm in Job—and in all the magnificent parts of the Old Testament. You hear it in that double way of saying a thing, that the Hebrews used.—It is said— then said right off again—a little differently," as Mary recorded in her Journal on 19 May 1922.

AND ONE WHO had served in the Temple besought him saying: "Teach us, Master, that our words may be even as your words, a chant and an incense unto the people."

And Almustafa answered and said: "You shall rise beyond your words, but your path shall remain, a rhythm and a fragrance; a rhythm for lovers and for all who are beloved, and a fragrance for those who would live life in a garden.

"But you shall rise beyond your words to a summit whereon the stardust falls, and you shall open your hands until they are filled; then you shall lie down and sleep like a white fledgling in a white nest, and you shall dream of your tomorrow as white violets dream of spring.

"Ay, and you shall go down deeper than your words. You shall seek the lost fountainheads of the streams, and you shall be a hidden cave echoing the faint voices of the depths which now you do not even hear.

"You shall go down deeper than your words, ay, deeper than all sounds, to the very heart of the earth, and there you shall be alone with Him who walks also upon the Milky Way."

From *The Garden of the Prophet*, 1933

Detail from *The Madman (When the sun kissed his own naked face for the first time)*, 1918, Pencil,
8¼ x 11 inches (28 x 21 cm), Gibran Museum, Bisharri, Lebanon

For it is Sufficient Unto the Hour

IN THE CONCLUDING words to *A Tear and a Smile*, published in 1914, Gibran wrote, "I came to say a word and shall utter it. Should death take me ere I give voice, the morrow shall utter it. For the morrow leaves not a secret hidden in the book of the Infinite." He wrote with similar sentiment to May Ziadeh in Cairo in the late 1920s, expressing his fears lest he died before he could utter that word. Gibran had actually planned a trilogy: *The Prophet*, *The Garden of the Prophet* and *The Death of the Prophet*. He had much of the second volume written before his death, but it was his literary executor, Barbara Young (see page 206), who gathered together the work and published it posthumously, in 1933. Nothing but a short fragment remains of the third work in the projected trilogy: "And he shall return to the City of Orphalese, and they shall stone him in the marketplace, even unto death; and he shall call every stone a blessed name." By 1996, *The Prophet* had sold nine million copies in North America alone since its first publication in 1923, and it had been translated into almost forty languages.

And Almustafa advanced and met them upon the road, and they passed through the gate, and all was well, as though they had gone their path but an hour ago.

They came in and supped with him at his frugal board, after that Karima had laid upon it the bread and the fish and poured the last of the wine into the cups. And as she poured, she besought the Master saying: "Give me leave that I go into the city and fetch wine to replenish your cups, for this is spent."

And he looked upon her, and in his eyes were a journey and a far country, and he said: "Nay, for it is sufficient unto the hour."

And they ate and drank and were satisfied. And when it was finished, Almustafa spoke in a vast voice, deep as the sea and full as a great tide under the moon, and he said: "My comrades and my road fellows, we must needs part this day. Long have we sailed the perilous seas, and we have climbed the steepest mountains and we have wrestled with the storms. We have known hunger, but we have also sat at wedding feasts. Oftentimes have we been naked, but we have also worn kingly raiment. We have indeed traveled far, but now we part. Together you shall go your way, and alone must I go mine.

"And though the seas and the vast lands shall separate us, still we shall be companions upon our journey to the Holy Mountain.

"But before we go our severed roads, I would give unto you the harvest and the gleaning of my heart:

"Go you upon your way with singing, but let each song be brief, for only the songs that die young upon your lips shall live in human hearts.

"Tell a lovely truth in little words, but never an ugly truth in any words. Tell the maiden whose hair shines in the sun that she is the daughter of the morning. But if you shall behold the sightless, say not to him that he is one with night.

"Listen to the flute player as it were listening to April, but if you shall hear the critic and the fault finder speak, be deaf as your own bones and as distant as your fancy.

"My comrades and my beloved, upon your way you shall meet men with hoofs; give them your wings. And men with horns; give them wreaths of laurel. And men with claws; give them petals for fingers. And men with forked tongues; give them honey for words.

"Ay, you shall meet all these and more; you shall meet the lame selling crutches; and the blind, mirrors. And you shall meet the rich men begging at the gate of the Temple.

"To the lame give of your swiftness, to the blind of your vision; and see that you give of yourself to the rich beggars; they are the most needy of all, for surely no man would stretch a hand for alms unless he be poor indeed, though of great possessions.

"My comrades and my friends, I charge you by our love that you be countless paths which cross one another in the desert, where the lions and the rabbits walk, and also the wolves and the sheep.

"And remember this of me: I teach you not giving, but receiving; not denial, but fulfilment; and not yielding, but understanding, with the smile upon the lips.

"I teach you not silence, but rather a song not overloud.

"I teach you your larger self, which contains all men."

And he rose from the board and went out straightway into the Garden and walked under the shadow of the cypress trees as the day waned. And they followed him, at a little distance, for their heart was heavy, and their tongue clave to the roof of their mouth.

Only Karima, after she had put by the fragments, came unto him and

said: "Master, I would that you suffer me to prepare food against the morrow and your journey."

And he looked upon her with eyes that saw other worlds that this, and he said: "My sister, and my beloved, it is done, even from the beginning of time. The food and the drink is ready, for the morrow, even as for our yesterday and our today.

"I go, but if I go with a truth not yet voiced, that very truth will again seek me and gather me, though my elements be scattered throughout the silences of eternity, and again shall I come before you that I may speak with a voice born anew out of the heart of those boundless silences.

"And if there be aught of beauty that I have declared not unto you, then once again shall I be called, ay, even by mine own name, Almustafa, and I shall give you a sign, that you may know I have come back to speak all that is lacking, for God will not suffer Himself to be hidden from man, nor His word to lie covered in the abyss of the heart of man.

"I shall live beyond death, and I shall sing in your ears
Even after the vast sea wave carries me back
To the vast sea depth.
I shall sit at your board though without a body,
And I shall go with you to your fields, a spirit invisible.
I shall come to you at your fireside, a guest unseen.
Death changes nothing but the masks that cover our faces.
The woodsman shall be still a woodsman,
The ploughman, a ploughman,
And he who sang his song to the wind shall sing it also to the
    moving spheres."

And the disciples were as still as stones, and grieved in their heart for that he had said: "I go." But no man put out his hand to stay the Master, nor did any follow after his footsteps.

And Almustafa went out from the Garden of his mother, and his feet were swift and they were soundless; and in a moment, like a blown leaf in a strong wind, he was far gone from them, and they saw, as it were, a pale light moving up to the heights.

And the nine walked their ways down the road. But the woman still stood in the gathering night, and she beheld how the light and the twilight were become one; and she comforted her desolation and her aloneness with his words: "I go, but if I go with a truth not yet voiced, that very truth will seek me and gather me, and again shall I come."

From *The Garden of the Prophet,* 1933

O Mist, My Sister

GIBRAN FANTASIZED for years with Mikhail Naimy about purchasing the beautiful, serene Mar Sarkis Monastery in Bisharri, so that they could retire and spend the rest of their days in the joys of solitude, writing and painting. Sadly, it would only be Gibran's final resting place. The sign on the entrance features one word in Arabic on which the dots on the characters have curiously shifted place to create a telling ambiguity. The sign reads both "Here lies *among us* Gibran" and "Here lies *our Prophet* Gibran!" Gibran confided in Mary Haskell on 12 August 12 1921, some ten years before his death, "I sometimes imagine myself, my bodily part, after death, lying in the earth and returning to the elements of earth: the great loosening, the change everywhere, the opening into simpler things, the widening out into those things from which anything may be built up again, the great Return, such deep quietness and a passing into the substance of things." In his will, Gibran was mindful of those close to him. To his sister Mariana, he left money, shares and securities. Everything in "The Hermitage" in New York— his books, pictures, objets d'art and manuscripts—he bequeathed to Mary Haskell, as he had promised. The royalties from his copyrights were donated to his home village.

AND NOW IT was eventide.
And he had reached the hills. His steps had led him to the mist, and he stood among the rocks and the white cypress trees hidden from all things, and he spoke and said:

"O Mist, my sister, white breath not yet held in a mold,
I return to you, a breath white and voiceless,
A word not yet uttered.

"O Mist, my wingèd sister mist, we are together now,
And together we shall be till life's second day,
Whose dawn shall lay you, dewdrops in a garden,
And me a babe upon the breast of a woman,
And we shall remember.

"O Mist, my sister, I come back, a heart listening in its
	depths,
Even as your heart,
A desire throbbing and aimless even as your desire,
A thought not yet gathered, even as your thought.

"O Mist, my sister, firstborn of my mother,
My hands still hold the green seeds you bade me scatter,
And my lips are sealed upon the song you bade me sing;
And I bring you no fruit, and I bring you no echoes
For my hands were blind, and my lips unyielding.

"O Mist, my sister, much did I love the world, and the
	world loved me,

For all my smiles were upon her lips, and all her tears were in my eyes.
Yet there was between us a gulf of silence which she would not abridge
And I could not overstep.

"O Mist, my sister, my deathless sister Mist,
I sang the ancient songs unto my little children,
And they listened, and there was wondering upon their face;
But tomorrow perchance they will forget the song,
And I know not to whom the wind will carry the song.
And though it was not mine own, yet it came to my heart
And dwelt for a moment upon my lips.

"O Mist, my sister, though all this came to pass,
I am at peace.
It was enough to sing to those already born.
And though the singing is indeed not mine,
Yet it is of my heart's deepest desire.

"O Mist, my sister, my sister Mist,
I am one with you now.
No longer am I a self.
The walls have fallen,
And the chains have broken;
I rise to you, a mist,
And together we shall float upon the sea until life's second day,
When dawn shall lay you, dewdrops in a garden,
And me a babe upon the breast of a woman."

From *The Garden of the Prophet,* 1933

KAHLIL GIBRAN TIMELINE

1883
Kahlil Gibran is born Gibran Khalil Gibran on 6 January in Bisharri into a Maronite Catholic family.

1885
Gibran's first sister, Mariana, is born.

1887
Gibran's sister, Sultana, is born.

1891
Gibran's father, Kahlil Gibran, is jailed for tax evasion.

1895
Mother Kamila and her four children, including Gibran's half-brother Peter, emigrate to Boston's South End, USA. Peter opens a small shop; Gibran joins the Quincy Public School.

1897
Gibran meets photographer and artist Fred Holland Day, and poses for various photographic studies. Through Day he meets the young poet Josephine Preston Peabody.

1898
Gibran returns to Lebanon to study Arabic at the famous *Madrasat al-Hikma*, School of Wisdom, in Beirut.

1902
Gibran returns to Boston, arriving shortly after Sultana's death from tuberculosis.

1903
Peter dies of tuberculosis in March; Kamila dies of cancer in June. Gibran begins a relationship with Josephine Peabody, who would arrange his first exhibition at Wellesley College, Massachusetts.

1904
Gibran stages an exhibition at Fred Holland Day's studio and meets Mary Elizabeth Haskell, who exhibits Gibran's art at her Cambridge School.

1906
Gibran publishes *'Ara'is al-muruj* (Nymphs of the Valley).

1908
Al-arwah al-mutamarrida (Spirits Rebellious) is published. Gibran moves to Paris to study art.

1911
Gibran meets Abdul Bahá, son of the leader of the Bahá'í Faith. He writes a political draft in support of Syria.

1912
Al-ajniha al-mutakassira (The Broken Wings) is published. Gibran moves to New York. W. B. Yeats agrees to sit for his "Temple of Art" series, as does Carl Gustav Jung a year later.

1914
Dam'a wa ibtisama (A Tear and a Smile) is published; Gibran exhibits paintings and drawings at The Montross Galleries in New York.

1916
Gibran meets Mikhail Naimy and Rabindranath Tagore, who sits for Gibran's "Temple of Art" series.

1918
Gibran publishes *The Madman: His Parables and Poems*.

1919
Twenty Drawings and the long poem *al-Mawakib* (The Processions) are published.

1920
Al-'awasif (The Tempests) and *The Forerunner: His Parables and Poems* are published. Gibran founds *Arrabitah*, the New York Pen Club, with other Arab expatriate writers.

1923
Gibran publishes *The Prophet* and *al-Bada'i' wa al-tara'if* (Best Things and Masterpieces). His health declines.

1926
Sand and Foam is published.

1927
Kalimat Gibran (The Words of Gibran) is published.

1928
Jesus, Son of Man is published.

1929
Al-sanabil (The Spikes of Grain) is published.

1931
The Earth Gods is published. Gibran dies from tuberculosis and liver disease on 10 April. After his funeral in Boston, the body is laid to rest in the Mar Sarkis Monastery in Bisharri.

1932
Gibran's completed work, *The Wanderer: His Parables and Sayings*, is published posthumously.

1933
Gibran's unfinished sequel to *The Prophet* is published under *The Garden of the Prophet*.

1981
Gibran's two plays, *Lazarus and His Beloved* and *The Blind*, are published.

BIBLIOGRAPHY

Works by Kahlil Gibran

Nubdha fi fann al-musiqa (On Music, a Pamphlet). New York: Al-Mohajer, 1905.

'Ara'is al-muruj (Brides of the Meadows). New York: Al-Mohajer, 1906. Trans. H. M. NAHMAD as *Nymphs of the Valley* (New York: Alfred A. Knopf, 1948), and by J. R. I. COLE as *Spirit Brides* (Ashland: White Cloud Press, 1993).

Al-arwah al-mutamarrida (Spirits Rebellious). New York: Al-Mohajer, 1908. Trans. H. M. NAHMAD as *Spirits Rebellious* (New York: Alfred A. Knopf, 1948).

Al-ajniha al-mutakassira (The Broken Wings). New York: Mir'at al-Gharb, 1912. Trans. A. R. FERRIS as *The Broken Wings* (New York: Citadel Press, 1957), and by J. R. I. COLE as *The Broken Wings* (Santa Cruz: White Cloud Press, 1998).

Dum'a wa ibtisama (A Tear and a Smile). New York: Atlantic, 1914. Trans. A. R. FERRIS as *Tears and Laughter* (New York: Philosophical Library, 1947), and by H. M. NAHMAD as *A Tear and a Smile* (New York: Alfred A. Knopf, 1950).

The Madman: His Parables and Poems. New York: Alfred A. Knopf, 1918.

Al-mawakib (The Processions). New York: Mir'at al-Gharb, 1919. Trans. M. F. KHEIRALLAH as *The Processions* (New York: Arab-American Press, 1947).

Twenty Drawings. New York: Alfred A. Knopf, 1919.

Al-'awasif (The Tempests). Cairo: Dar al-Hilal, 1920. Trans. in selections by ANDREW GHAREEB as Prose Poems (New York: Alfred A. Knopf, 1934), and by JOHN WALBRIDGE as The Storm: Stories and Prose Poems (Santa Cruz: White Cloud Press, 1993).

The Forerunner: His Parables and Poems. New York: Alfred A. Knopf, 1920.

Al-bada'i' wa al-tara'if (Best Things and Masterpieces). Cairo: Yusuf Bustani, 1923.

The Prophet. New York: Alfred A. Knopf, 1923.

Sand and Foam. New York: Alfred A. Knopf, 1926.

Kalimat Gibran (The Words of Gibran). Cairo: Yusuf Bustani, 1927. Trans. A. R. FERRIS as *Spiritual Sayings* (New York: Citadel Press, 1962).

Jesus, The Son of Man. New York: Alfred A. Knopf, 1928.

Al-sanabil (The Spikes of Grain). New York: Al-Sa'ih, 1929.

The Earth Gods. New York: Alfred A. Knopf, 1931.

The Wanderer: His Parables and Sayings. New York: Alfred A. Knopf, 1932.

The Garden of the Prophet. New York: Alfred A. Knopf, 1933.

Lazarus and His Beloved and The Blind. Philadelphia: Westminister Press, 1981.

Paintings and Drawings 1905–1930. New York: Vrej Baghoomian, 1989.

Editions and Anthologies

The Beloved: Reflections on the Path of the Heart, trans. JOHN WALBRIDGE. Ashland: White Cloud Press, 1994.

Between Night and Morn: A Special Selection, trans. A. R. FERRIS. New York: Wisdom Library, 1972.

The Collected Works. New York: Alfred A. Knopf, 2007.

Gibran in His Museum, eds. WAHIB KAYROUZ. Bisharri: Bacharia, 1999.

Kahlil Gibran (1883–1931): Horizons of the Painter, eds. SYLVIA AGEMIAN and WAHIB KAYROUZ. Beirut: Nicolas Sursock Museum and Gibran Museum, 2000.

The Eye of the Prophet, trans. M. CROSLAND. London: Souvenir Press, 1995.

An Introduction to the Art of Kahlil Gibran. New York: Alpine Fine Arts Collection, 1991.

The Kahlil Gibran Reader: Inspirational Writings. Secaucus, NJ: Carol Publishing Group, 1995.

Mirrors of the Soul, trans. JOSEPH SHEBAN. Secaucus, NJ: Castle Books, 1993.

Sculpture: Kahlil Gibran. Forward by E. H. TURNER. Boston: Bartlett Press, 1970.

A Second Treasury of Kahlil Gibran, ed. M. L. WOLF and trans. A. R. FERRIS. New York: Citadel Press, 1962.

Thoughts and Meditations, trans. A. R. FERRIS. New York: Citadel Press, 1961.

A Third Treasury of Kahlil Gibran, ed. A. D. SHERFAN. Secaucus, NJ: Citadel Press, 1975.

A Treasury of Kahlil Gibran, ed. M. L. WOLF, trans. A R. FERRIS. New York: Citadel Press, 1951.

The Vision: Reflections on the Way of the Soul, trans. J. R. I. COLE. Ashland: White Cloud Press, 1994.

The Voice of Kahlil Gibran, ed. R. WATERFIELD. London: Penguin, 1995.

The Voice of the Master, trans. A R. FERRIS. New York: Citadel Press, 1963.

The Wisdom of Gibran: *Aphorisms and Maxims,* ed. and trans. JOSEPH SHEBAN. New York: Philosophical Library, 1966.

Biographies and Letters

BUSHRUI, S. B. and S. H. AL-KUZBARI, eds. and trans. *Blue Flame: The Love Letters of Kahlil Gibran and May Ziadah.* Harlow: Longman, 1983.

BUSHRUI, S. B. and S. H. AL-KUZBARI, eds. and trans. *Gibran: Love Letters.* Oxford: Oneworld, 1995.

BUSHRUI, SUHEIL and JOE JENKINS. *Kahil Gibran: Man and Poet, A New Biography.* Oxford: Oneworld, 1998.

FERRIS, A. R., ed. and trans. *Gibran, A Self-Portrait.* New York: The Citadel Press, 1969.

GIBRAN, JEAN AND KAHLIL GIBRAN. *Kahlil Gibran, His Life and World.* Edinburgh: Canongate Press, 1992; 1974.

HILU, VIRGINIA, ed. and trans. *Beloved Prophet: The Love Letters of Kahil Gibran and Mary Haskell, and Her Private Journal.* New York: Alfred A. Knopf, 1971.

HUWAYYIK, YUSUF. *Gibran in Paris.* New York: Popular Library, 1976.

NAIMY, MIKHAIL. *Kahlil Gibran, A Biography.* New York: Quartet Books, 1988; 1934.

NAJJAR, ALEXANDER. *Kahil Gibran, A Biography,* trans. RAE AZKOUL. London: Saqi Books, 2008.

WATERFIELD, ROBIN. *Prophet: The Life and Times of Kahil Gibran.* New York: St. Martin's Press, 1998.

YOUNG, BARBARA. *This Man from Lebanon: A Study of Kahlil Gibran.* New York: Alfred A. Knopf, 1971; 1945.

Further Reading

AKARLI, ENGIN D. *The Long Peace: Ottoman Lebanon 1861–1920.* Berkeley: University of California Press, 1993.

ALLEN, ROGER. *The Arabic Literary Heritage: The Development of its Genres and Criticism.* Cambridge: Cambridge University Press, 1998.

ARBERRY, A. J. *Sufism: An Account of the Mystics of Islam.* London: Unwin, 1990.

BADAWI, M. M. *A Critical Introduction to Modern Arabic Poetry.* Cambridge: University Press, 1975.

BARFIELD, OWEN. *Saving the Appearances, A Study in Idolatry.* New York: Harcourt Brace Janovich, 1976.

BAUERLEIN, MARK. *Whitman and the American Idiom.* Baton Rouge: Louisiana State University Press, 1991.

BLACKMUR, R. P. *Language as Gesture: Essays in Poetry.* New York: Harcourt, Brace and Company, 1952.

BOWRA, MAURICE. *The Romantic Imagination.* Cambridge, MA: Harvard University Press, 1950.

BRADFORD, GAMALIEL. *A Naturalist of Souls: Studies in Psychography.* Port Washington, NY: Kennikat Press, 1926; 1969.

BRECKMAN, WARREN. *European Romanticism: A Brief History with Documents.* Bedford: St Martin's 2007.

BUELL, LAWRENCE. *The American Transcendentalists: Essential Writings.* New York: Modern Library, 2006.

BUSHRUI, S. B., J. M. MUNROE, M. SMITH and S. A. HAMDEH, eds. *A Poet and his Country: Gibran's Lebanon.* Beirut: Middle East Press Inc., 1970.

BUSHRUI, S. B. and P. GOTCH, eds. *Gibran of Lebanon: New Papers.* Beirut: Librairie du Liban, 1975.

BUSHRUI, S. B. and J. M. MUNROE, eds. *Kahlil Gibran: Essays and Introductions.* Beirut: Rihani House, 1970.

BYNNER, WITTER. "Kahlil the Gibranite," *in the Borzoi: Being a Sort of Record of Ten Years' Publishing.* New York: Knopf, 1925, pp. 43–46.

CAVITCH, DAVID. *My Soul and I: The Inner Life of Walt Whitman.* Boston: Beacon Press, 1985.

CHOWDHRY, SHIV RAJ. *Gibran: An Introduction.* Delhi: Javee and Co., 1970.

DAOUDI, M. S. *The Meaning of Kahlil Gibran.* Secaucus, NJ: Citadel Press, 1982.

DORRA, HENRI, ed. *Symbolist Art Theories.* Berkeley: University of California Press, 1994.

FRYE, NORTHROP. *Fearful Symmetry: A Study of William Blake.* Princeton: Princeton University Press, 1972.

GHOUGASSIAN, JOSEPH P. *Kahlil Gibran: Wings of Thought, The People's Philosopher.* New York: Philosophical Library, 1973.

HAWI, KHALIL S. *Kahlil Gibran: His Background, Character and Works.* Beirut: American University of Beirut, 1972.

HITTI, PHILIP K. *Lebanon in History from Earliest Times to the Present.* London: Macmillan, 1967.

HOOGLUND, ERIC J., ed. *Crossing the Waters: Arabic-Speaking Immigrants to the United States before 1940.* Washington, DC: Smithsonian Institute Press, 1987.

HOWE, M. A. DE WOLFE. *Boston: The Place and the People.* New York: Macmillan, 1903.

AL-JAYYUSI, SALMA AL-KHADRA. *Trends and Movements in Modern Arabic Poetry.* 2 vols. Leiden: E. J. Brill, 1977.

JUDAH, J. STILLSON. *The History and Philosophy of the Metaphysical Movements in America*. Philadelphia: Westminster Press, 1967.

JUNG, C. G. *Modern Man in Search of a Soul,* trans. W. S. DELL AND CARY F. BAYNES. New York: Harcourt Brace & Company, 1933.

KAZANTZAKIS, NIKOS. *The Odyssey; A Modern Sequel,* trans. KIMON FRIAR. New York: Simon and Schuster, 1958.

KAZANTZAKIS, NIKOS. *Report to Greco,* trans. P. A. BIEN. New York: Simon & Schuster, INC., 1965.

KNOPF, ALFRED A. *Portrait of a Publisher 1915–1965*: *Reminiscences and Reflections,* 2 vols. New York: Typophiles, 1965.

LASCH, CHRISTOPHER. *The New Radicalism in America (1889–1963)*. New York: Knopf, 1965.

MOREH, S. *Modern Arabic Poetry 1800–1970: The Development of its Forms and Themes under the Influence of Western Literature*. Leiden: E. J. Brill, 1976.

NIETZSCHE, FRIEDRICH. *Thus Spoke Zarathustra,* trans. R. J. HOLLINGDALE. New York: Penguin Books, 1985.

OTTO, ANNIE SALEM. *The Art of Kahlil Gibran: Visions of Life as Expressed by the Author of* The Prophet. Port Arthur: Hinds, 1965.

OTTO, ANNIE SALEM. *The Parables of Kahlil Gibran: An Interpretation of His Writings and Art*. New York: the Citadel Press, 1963.

PETERS, F. E. *Judaism, Christianity and Islam: The Classical Texts and their Interpretation,* 2 vols. Princeton: Princeton University Press, 1990.

RILKE, RAINER MARIA. *Neue Gedichte/New Poems,* trans. STEPHEN COHN. Manchester: Carcanet, 1997.

ROBERTS, RICHARD. *The Jesus of Poets and Prophets*. London: Student Christian Movement, 1919.

ROSTON, MURRAY. *Prophet and Poet: The Bible and the Growth of Romanticism*. New York: Faber and Faber, 1965.

SHARABI, HISHAM. *Arab Intellectuals and the West: The Formative Years, 1875–1914*. Baltimore: Johns Hopkins University Press, 1970.

SHEHADI, WILLIAM. *Kahlil Gibran: A Prophet in the Making*. Syracuse: Syracuse University Press, 1992.

SHERFAN, ANDREW DIB. *Kahlil Gibran: The Nature of Love*. New York: Philosophical Library, 1971.

STEVENS, ETHEL S. *Cedars, Saints and Sinners in Syria*. London: Hurst and Blackett, 1927.

THURBON, COLIN. *The Hills of Adonis*. London: Heinemann, 1968.

WAGNER, WILLIAM F. *The Life and Writings of Kahlil Gibran: An Analysis and Theological Interpretation*. Martinsville, IN: Airleaf Publishing, 2006.

WARE, CAROLINE. *Greenwich Village 1920–1930*. Boston: Houghton Mifflin, 1935.

WHITMAN, WALT. *Leaves of Grass: The Inclusive Edition,* eds. EMORY HOLLOWAY, et. al. Garden City, NY: Doubleday & Company, INC., 1926.

WILSON, EDMUND. *The Shores of Light*: A Literary Chronicle of the Twenties and Thirties. New York: Farrar, Straus and Young, 1952.

YOUNG, BRAD H. *The Parables: Jewish Tradition and Christian Interpretation*. Peabody, MA: Hendrickson Publishers, 1998.

INDEX

ACKNOWLEDGMENTS

This Anthology would have remained in the silent unsaid of Kahlil Gibran's universe had it not been for the vision and dedication of the editorial team at Spruce. Ljiljana Baird, publisher, was the first to conceive of this elegant home for Gibran's scattered offspring of the spirit, and, ever mindful, saw the edifice rising block by block to the tally of the vision befitting of a Gibran homecoming. Camilla Davis, managing editor, has been ever watchful, waiting at every rung of the ladder, urging the ascent, yet ever so kindly. Kate Fox, editorial assistant, saw ever so skilfully to the cementing blocks. To Susannah Marriott, copy editor, I am most grateful for the many revisions and sharp insights into questions of syntax and voice, and to the designer, Carole Ash, I am grateful.

My thanks go to colleagues at SOAS for their support during my sabbatical leave: Michael Hutt, Stefan Sperl, Muhammad Said, and especially Grace E. Koh, for giving so generously of her time and energy. Also to Savitri Sperl, Barbara Bouman and Emma Parsons for their never failing support.

The completion of this book coincided with the commemoration of the passages of father, sister Safiyya and brother Muhammad; to them and to mother, Suad Mejahid, sisters, Mona and Amany, and brothers Ibrahim and Mohie, and their wonderful spouses and offspring, this book is also dedicated.

The Publisher and I would also like to thank the **Kahlil Gibran Estate** and the **Kahlil Gibran Educational Fund** for all their support and for helping make this book possible.

PICTURE ACKNOWLEDGMENTS

The publishers would like to thank **Walid Nasser & Associates**, Beirut, Lebanon, for providing the majority of images in this book, with the authorisation of the Gibran National Committee, PO Box 116-5375, Beirut, Lebanon. Phone and facsimile (+961-1) 396916; e-mail k.gibran@cyberia.net.lb.

Other images were supplied by the following:

Bridgeman Art Library National Gallery of Scotland, Edinburgh 37; Private Collection 2; **Corbis** Bettmann 196; The Gallery Collection 118; **Science & Society Picture Library**; Royal Photographic Society 28; **Smithsonian Institution, Washington DC**; Smithsonian American Art Museum/Peter A. Juley & Son Collection 33, 190; **Telfair Museum of Art, Savannah, GA** photos by Erwin Gaspin 34, 50, 114, 142, 154, 174; **Writer Pictures**: F. Holland Day/LOC 26.